COUNTRY STUDIES

SOUTH AFRICA

Garrett Nagle
Series Editor: John Hopkin

Heinemann Library,
Halley Court, Jordan Hill, Oxford OX2 8EJ
A division of Reed Educational & Professional Publishing Ltd.
Heinemann is a registered trademark of Reed Educational & Professional Publishing

OXFORD MELBOURNE AUCKLAND
JOHANNESBURG BALANTYRE GABORONE
IBADAN PORTSMOUTH (NH) USA CHICAGO
© Garrett Nagle
The moral right of the proprietor has been asserted

First published 1998

02 01 00 99 98
10 9 8 7 6 5 4 3 2 1

British Library Cataloguing in Publication Data

Nagle, Garrett
  South Africa. – (Country studies)
  1. South Africa – Social conditions – 1961 – – Juvenile literature
  2. South Africa – History – 1961 – – Juvenile literature
  3. South Africa – Description and travel
  I. Title
  968'.06

ISBN 0 431 01414 0 (Hardback)
     0 431 01415 9 (Paperback)

Typeset and illustrated by Hardlines, Charlbury, Oxford OX7 3PS
Printed and bound in Spain by Mateu Cromo

For Angela, Rosie and Patrick

Acknowledgements
The publishers would like to thank the following for permission to reproduce copyright material.

Maps and extracts
p.5 B, C,40 B Jutas General School Atlas, 1996, Juta & Co Ltd, South Africa Atlas; **p.10 B** Reed International; **p.11 C** Development Bank of Southern Africa; **p.14 B, C** Barnard, Smit and Van Zyl (after Jordaan); **p.25 C** *Geographical Magazine*; **p.27 D** Whitehead & O'Donovan (HSRC); **p.30 B** Paul Chapman Publishing, London; **p.33 C** © Crown Copyright Ordnance Survey; **p.38 B** Reed International; **p.39 E** *Financial Times*; **p.40 C** Consolidated Gold Fields Plc; **p.52 B** *Financial Times*; **p.53 D** Geographical; **p.57 D** Heinemann Educational.

Photographs
p.6 B SIPA-Press/Rex Features; **p.6 C** N Durrell McKenna/Hutchison Library; **p.6 D** Richard Lord/Rex Features; **p.14 A** SIPA-Press /Rex Features; **p.16 A** Tim Lambon/Environmental Images; **p.16 D** Paul Weinberg/Panos Pictures; **p.18 A** Bradley Arden/Panos Pictures; **p.30 A** Chris Sattleberger/Panos Pictures; **p.30 C** Mark Peters/Rex Features; **p.33 D** Axis; **p.39 F** Charles Ward/Camera Press; **p.41 D** Rodney Bond/Camera Press; **p.43 C** Jan Kope/Camera Press; **p.43 D** Paul Weinberg/Panos Pictures; **p.44 C** S Burman/Hutchison Library; **p.46 C** Daphne Christelis/Environmental Images; **p.47 D** Vanessa Burger/Images of Africa Photobank; **p.48 A** Gareth Boden; **p.52 A** Clive Shirley/Environmental Images; **p.54 A** David Reed/Panos Pictures; **p.55 B** M Kahn/Hutchison Library; **p.55 C** Geoslides; **p.58 A** Anders Gunnartz/Panos Pictures; **p.58 C** SIPA-Press/Rex Features; all other photographs courtesy of the author.
Cover: Getty Images; Eye Ubiquitous/Skjold

Contents

1 Introducing South Africa

A world in one country   4–5
Perceptions of South Africa   6–7
South Africa and apartheid   8–9

2 Physical environments

The effect of relief   10–11
South Africa's climate   12–13
River's, floods and irrigation   14–15
Environmental issues in South Africa   16–17
Drought and desertification   18–19
Investigation: Desertification and soil
  erosion in the Eastern Cape   20–21

3 Human environments

South Africa's population   22–23
Population change   24–25
Measuring development in
  South Africa   26–27
Migration in South Africa   28–29
Urbanization and inequality   30–31
Investigation: Rural settlement   32–33
Investigation: A black township,
  Fingo Village, Grahamstown   34–35

4 Economic environments

The two sides of South African
  agriculture   36–37
Manufacturing and economic change   38–39
Gold mining: an industry under threat   40–41
Closing the energy gap   42–43
Tourism   44–45
Investigation: Private game parks:
  making the best of South Africa's
  dry areas?   46–47
South Africa and international trade   48–49
Investigation: Black people developing
  the rural economy   50–51

5 Unequal regions

Measuring regional inequalities   52–53
The core region   54–55
South Africa's periphery   56–57
Investigation: Issues for the
  twenty-first century   58–59

Statistics   60–61
Glossary   62–63
Index   64

1 INTRODUCING SOUTH AFRICA

A world in one country

▶ **Where is South Africa?**
▶ **Why is it so different?**

South Africa is a very large country. It stretches from **latitude** 22° south to nearly 35° south, and from **longitude** 33° east to 17° east, covering an area of 1 221 000 km² . By contrast, the UK only covers an area of 244 000 km² (map **B**).

South Africa is also a very varied country. There are great contrasts in relief and distance from the sea, as well as latitude (map **B**). These cause big variations in the climate and vegetation, so there is a mixture of desert and semi-desert, grassland, Mediterranean, mountain and sub-tropical environments.

There are nine provinces in South Africa. The smallest one, Gauteng, contains the cities of Johannesburg and Pretoria. By contrast, the largest provinces, such as the Northern Cape, contain large areas of desert.

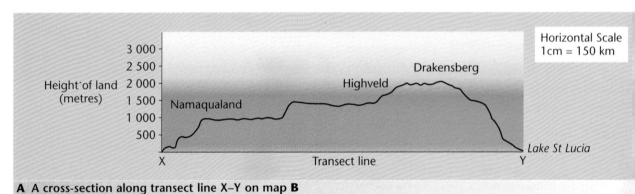

A A cross-section along transect line X–Y on map **B**

FACT FILE

Map projections

Although the Earth is a spherical body, maps show it as a two-dimensional object, with linear scales for latitude and longitude. This has the effect of increasing the relative importance of some areas, such as Greenland, and reducing the importance of others, especially African countries such as South Africa. Other projections, such as the Mollweide and the Sanson-Flamsteed, have cylindrical scales which reduce the importance of polar areas and give greater consideration to tropical areas.

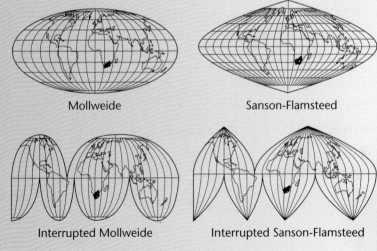

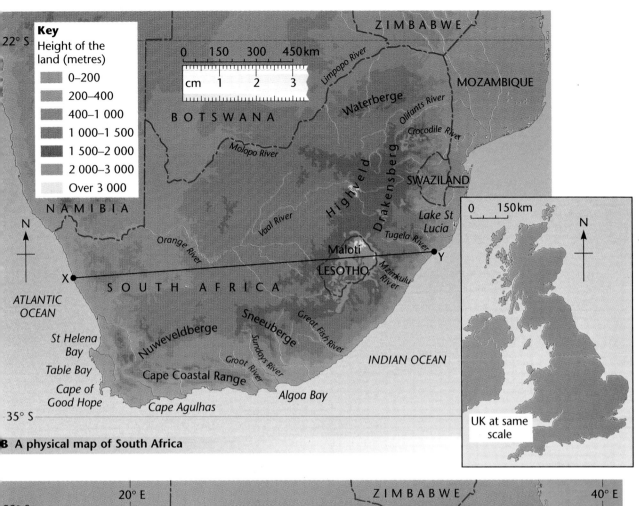

Key
Height of the
land (metres)

- 0–200
- 200–400
- 400–1 000
- 1 000–1 500
- 1 500–2 000
- 2 000–3 000
- Over 3 000

UK at same scale

B A physical map of South Africa

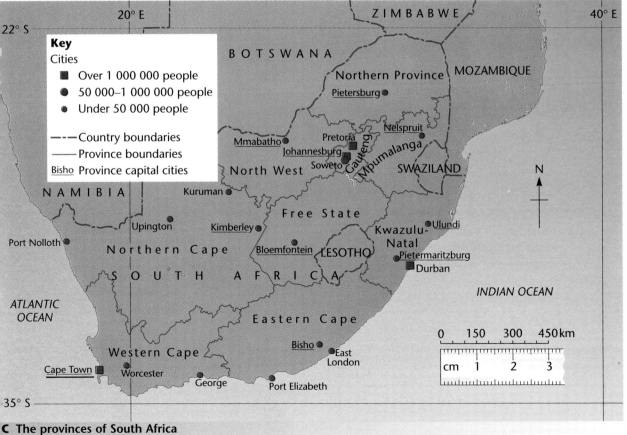

Key
Cities

- ■ Over 1 000 000 people
- ● 50 000–1 000 000 people
- • Under 50 000 people

-·—·- Country boundaries
—— Province boundaries
Bisho Province capital cities

C The provinces of South Africa

▶ **What do people think of South Africa?**
▶ **Why are there so many different viewpoints?**

Tourist

'South Africa was brilliant. It was really cheap, the beaches were excellent, the weather was hot and sunny, and there was so much to do and to see. We visited Kruger National Park and saw the 'big five': lion, rhino, elephant, buffalo, leopard. We also went to Cape Town and toured along the wine route, and we even did a tour of a **township**. Some people warned us that it would be dangerous, but we did not have any problems. If you keep out of those areas it's fine. I can't wait to go back.'

A Elephants – part of the Big Five attractions

A school boy after a rugby tour

'We had a great rugby tour. We played at a number of schools, and they really looked after us well. The standard of their sport is very high. Most of the time our A-team was playing a mixture of their As and Bs – and they still won most of the matches! The ground was very hard, and they tackled us like devils. We were treated very well, and stayed at the students' homes. They all seem to be quite well off and have lots of security around their houses.'

B Rugby on one of South Africa's dry pitches

A young South African couple who have moved to London

'We had to leave. The crime rate was going up and up. It's no place to bring up our children. Cars are being held up in broad daylight in city centres. It used to be just in the townships but now it's all over. Maybe it's better in small towns and in the countryside but we can't afford to live there because there aren't any jobs! All the jobs are in Johannesburg.'

C Security at a wealthy residence, Johannesburg

An Eastern Cape resident

'We don't want any more promises. We are sick of all that talk. We need jobs, houses, clinics, schools, and running water, not words. That's why I voted for the government. But what have they done for us? Nothing! Why should the whites still have all South Africa's riches? We are all South Africans.'

E Poor quality housing in the Eastern Cape

A UK investor

'South Africa is an exciting new market, and it's got in-roads into the rest of Southern Africa. We are keen to invest there. There is a great deal of talent in the population – there is a real buzz of progress in the new South Africa. As people become better off the market will expand – we want to be in there first.'

D UK investment in South Africa: exploitation or economic cure?

FACT FILE

Perception

People base their views on what they think exists (their **perception**) rather than what actually exists. Sometimes a person's perception can be very close to reality, other times it bears little resemblance. In general we would expect a person's perception to be closer to reality the more experience they have.

Thus, someone who has not been to South Africa will have a very limited understanding of life in South Africa compared with someone living there. In addition, among South Africans a white person's perception of the country will differ from that of a black person. This is a result of education, experience, class, economic status, and outlook.

In some cases peoples' perceptions are limited because of the constraints within which they live. A person who cannot read or write and/or someone who has suffered physical or mental assault, and who has been denied access to education or health care, will have a different view on the possibilities and the constraints of living in a society, compared with someone who has not been **discriminated** against.

In South Africa, there are clear racial variations in the perception of opportunity and quality of life.

▶ **How has South Africa's history influenced its geography?**
▶ **What was the apartheid policy?**

Apartheid was a policy of racial **segregation** which helped the white minority to keep political power. Between 1948 and 1994 the white National Party used apartheid to discriminate against the rest of the population. Today, the population of 40 million people are of varied descent (see page 22).

The effects of apartheid

However, there had been racism and **discrimination** in South Africa for a long time before 1948. It took place at different levels or scales.

- At national level or large scale, **homelands** were created and large numbers of black people were forced to live in them.
- At an **urban** scale, separate townships or **locations** were created for black people, coloured people and Indians. These were always of much poorer quality than the housing available for whites.
- On a small scale, beaches, trains, parks, hospitals and post offices were segregated by race. It was illegal for black people to use white facilities.

Apartheid forcibly removed millions of black people from 'white' farmlands and from 'white' areas of towns into the homelands and townships. In the homelands, new shanty towns were created but many of them were very far from the nearest town or city. These were called **resettlement schemes** or **peri-urban** settlements.

In the peri-urban settlements facilities such as schools, health care, water, sanitation and transport were very basic. Most of the people in these places were very poor and did not have much opportunity of getting a job. So the younger men **migrated** to 'white' South Africa to work in the mines and factories, while the elderly, children, women and the sick had to remain in the homelands.

The end of apartheid

The apartheid regime was ended in 1994 with the first democratic elections, when all South Africans were able to vote for the first time. South Africa's first black president, Nelson Mandela, was elected. His mission is described in **D**.

A Housing in the black township of Zwelitsha, Eastern Cape

B A resettlement scheme, Glenmore, Eastern Cape

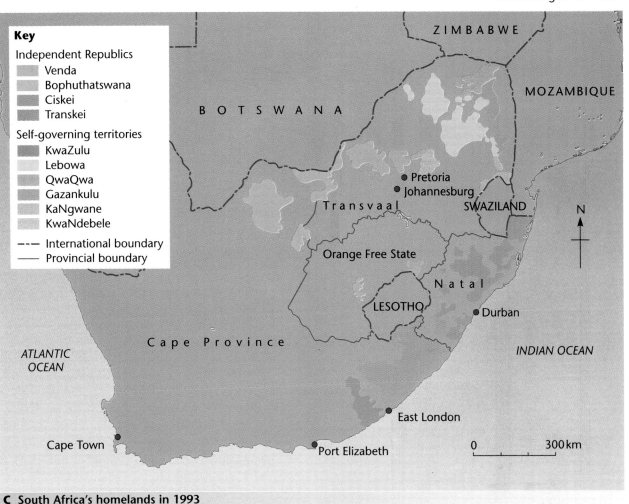

Key

Independent Republics
- Venda
- Bophuthatswana
- Ciskei
- Transkei

Self-governing territories
- KwaZulu
- Lebowa
- QwaQwa
- Gazankulu
- KaNgwane
- KwaNdebele

--- International boundary
— Provincial boundary

ZIMBABWE

MOZAMBIQUE

BOTSWANA

● Pretoria
● Johannesburg

Transvaal

SWAZILAND

N

Orange Free State

Natal

LESOTHO

● Durban

Cape Province

ATLANTIC OCEAN

INDIAN OCEAN

● East London

Cape Town ●

● Port Elizabeth

0   300 km

C South Africa's homelands in 1993

D NELSON MANDELA, *LONG WALK TO FREEDOM*, 1994

'I saw my mission as one of preaching reconciliation, of mending the wounds of the country. I knew that many people, particularly the minorities – whites, coloureds and Indians – would be feeling anxious about the future, and I wanted them to feel secure.'

FACT FILE

Dismantling apartheid

The South African government was put under a great deal of pressure by a number of governments and human rights organisations to end apartheid. Trade **sanctions** and disinvestment (the withdrawal of investment by foreign companies operating in South Africa) added pressure to the government to change.

However, the biggest challenge came from within South Africa, from among the black population and some liberal whites. Politically, the African National Congress (ANC) and the KwaZulu-dominated Inkatha group created a vocal political and military opposition. The churches of South Africa and the trade union movements also added their weight to the calls for a democratic future for all South Africans.

Between 1989 and 1994 apartheid was dismantled. Nelson Mandela was elected President of the Republic of South Africa after the first multi-racial democratic elections in South Africa were held in 1994.

2 PHYSICAL ENVIRONMENTS

The effect of relief

▶ **What are South Africa's main relief features?**
▶ **What influence do mountains have on climate and vegetation?**

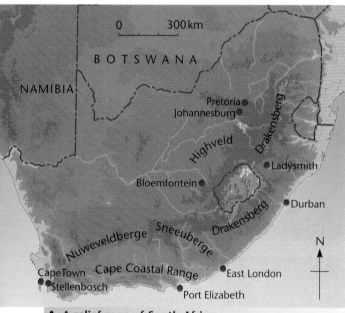

A A relief map of South Africa

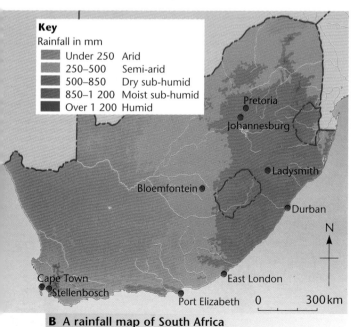

B A rainfall map of South Africa

South Africa has a number of important mountain ranges, including the Drakensberg, the Cape Coastal Range, the Sneeuberge and the Nuweveldberge. Much of the rest of South Africa is on a high **plateau**, the **Highveld** (**A**).

Relief has an important influence on climate in South Africa. In general, rainfall decreases from east to west, and over half of the country receives less than 250 mm of rain each year (**B**). Much of this rain is **relief rainfall**. As the air is forced to rise over a mountain, it cools and **condenses**. Clouds form and rain falls. For example, at the base of the Drakensberg near Ladysmith, annual rainfall is between 700 mm and 1 000 mm. At the top of the mountain it is almost 2 000 mm. Around Cape Town, rainfall in the lowland areas is just 400 mm. But in the mountains near Stellenbosch, less than 70 km away, it is as high as 3 000 mm each year.

Relief and slopes also affect the type of farming. On steep land, only rough grazing is possible. But in the flatter areas it is possible to grow crops where there is enough water.

In some areas, there are many sudden changes in relief. For example, in the Eastern Cape near Bisho, there are four main zones – a coastal plain, a deeply eroded plateau, a lowland basin, and the mountain belt. These have an important impact on local soils, weather and vegetation patterns.

For example, temperatures decrease with **altitude**. On average, for every 1 000 m of height the temperature falls by 10°C. So high mountain areas can be very cold, so that agriculture is more difficult here.

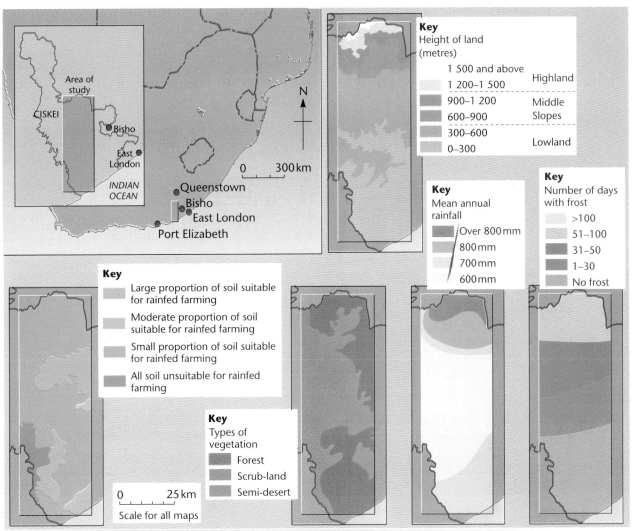

C Maps to show temperature, rainfall, vegetation and soils of an area near Bisho, Ciskei

Key
Height of land (metres)

1 500 and above	Highland
1 200–1 500	
900–1 200	Middle Slopes
600–900	
300–600	Lowland
0–300	

Key
Mean annual rainfall

- Over 800 mm
- 800 mm
- 700 mm
- 600 mm

Key
Number of days with frost

- >100
- 51–100
- 31–50
- 1–30
- No frost

Key

- Large proportion of soil suitable for rainfed farming
- Moderate proportion of soil suitable for rainfed farming
- Small proportion of soil suitable for rainfed farming
- All soil unsuitable for rainfed farming

Key
Types of vegetation

- Forest
- Scrub-land
- Semi-desert

Scale for all maps

FACT FILE

South Africa in relief

South Africa falls into three main topographic areas – the interior plateau, which contains large areas of land with an average elevation of 1200 m, the marginal lands which lie between the plateau and the coast, and the Great Escarpment which forms the border between the plateau and the marginal lands.

The marginal lands are more dissected (eroded) than the plateau and contain many rugged landscapes. The Escarpment contains the highest peaks within South Africa, Mont-aux-Sources at 2399 m, Champagne Castle at 3376 m, and Giant's Castle at 3313 m. The highest point in southern Africa is in the Great Escarpment but falls within Lesotho, Thabana-Ntlengana at 3482 m.

Key

- Kalahan Basin
- Plateau
- Marginal lands
- Coastal plains
- Mountains of the Great Escarpment
- Other mountains

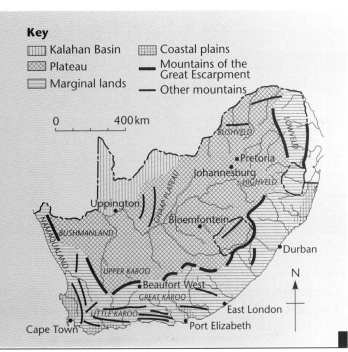

South Africa's climate

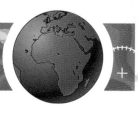

▶ Why has South Africa so many climates?
▶ How does climate vary in different seasons and different parts of the country?

South Africa is a country of many climates. It varies from place to place, as well as from season to season:

- rainfall is higher in the mountains (due to relief rainfall);
- rainfall decreases from east to west;
- most of the rainfall is in summer (October to March);
- the Cape Town area has rainfall in winter (April to September);
- temperatures increase away from the sea and northwards towards the Equator;
- temperatures are higher in lowland areas and cooler in the highlands.

Durban has a **sub-tropical** climate (graph **A**). It gets its climate from the warm Agulhas current. Summer temperatures are high (20°C–25°C) and the air is **humid** (sticky). Winters are warm (16°C–18°C) and frost free. Rainfall is about 1 000 mm, 70 per cent of it falling during the summer months. Some of this rainfall is very heavy and can cause serious soil erosion.

By contrast, Johannesburg is located on the **Highveld**. Summers are warm (about 20°C) although sometimes the temperatures can be much higher (30°C). Winters are mild (8°C–10°C) but the nights are very cold, and frosts are common. Temperatures are lower partly because of altitude. Up to 85 per cent of the rainfall occurs during the summer. Total annual rainfall is just over 800 mm (graph **B**). **Convection storms** (thunder storms) produce heavy rain and can cause local flooding.

The south-west corner of South Africa has a **Mediterranean climate** (graph **C**). Unlike other parts of the country, it has winter rainfall (April–September). Rainfall is moderate, about 600 mm, but can be as high as 3 000 mm in the mountains. Temperatures range from around 20°C in the summer to 15°C in winter. This is because the sea helps cool the coast in summer and warm it in winter.

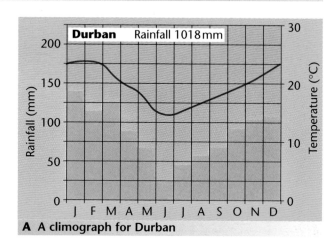

A A climograph for Durban

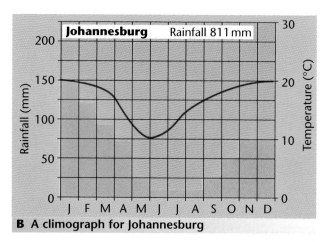

B A climograph for Johannesburg

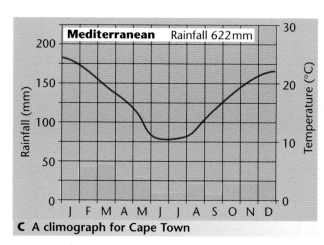

C A climograph for Cape Town

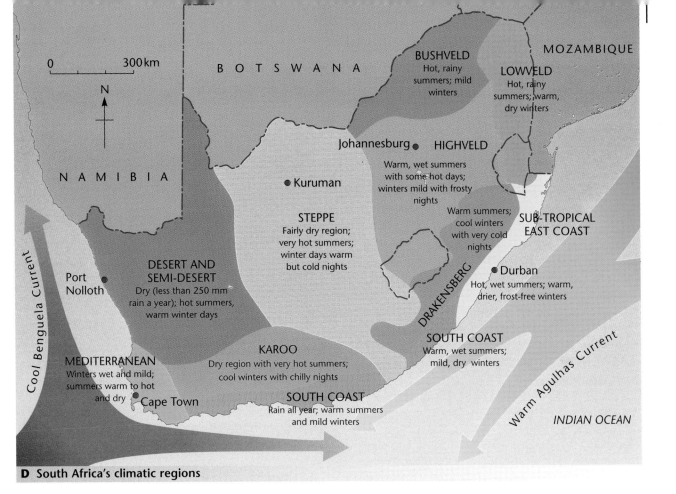

D South Africa's climatic regions

Kuruman is located in the Northern Cape, close to the border with the North West province. It has an interior location and is cut off from the modifying effect of the oceans. Summers are very hot and winters are very cold.

	J	F	M	A	M	J	J	A	S	O	N	D
Mean temperature	25	24	21	18	14	10	10	13	17	20	21	23
Precipitation	75	80	75	50	20	10	5	10	15	25	35	55
Total	455 mm											

E Climate data for Kuruman

FACT FILE

The effect of ocean currents
South Africa's **sub-tropical** location accounts for its warm temperatures. In addition, it falls within the belt of high pressure which generally provides dry conditions. Hence, its 'average' climate is one that is dry and warm. Nevertheless, the oceans on three of its four sides have a moderating effect.

These coasts act differently. On the east coast the warm Agulhas current raises temperatures, whereas on the west coast the cold Benguela current reduces temperatures. Thus,

there is a temperature difference of about 6°C between Durban (on the east coast) and Port Nolloth (on the west coast), despite them sharing the same **latitude**. The east coast areas are warmer and wetter. This is a result of the moister, unstable air over the warm Indian Ocean.

By contrast, over the west coast, air is chilled by the cold Benguela current and largely prevents rain from forming. Port Nolloth receives just 63 mm of rain a year, on average, compared with 1018 mm in Durban.

Rivers, floods and irrigation

> ▶ Why are there floods in South Africa as well as droughts?
> ▶ What can be done to help farmers overcome these hazards?

A Flash floods in KwaZulu-Natal, 1995

In South Africa, the variable climate causes a number of **natural hazards** which bring damage and destruction.
- Drought is a problem in many areas, especially for farmers.
- South Africa's rivers have great variations in their flows at different times of the year; at times there is not enough flow.
- At other times there is too much flow and flooding is a problem.

Floods do not occur at the same time throughout the country. For example, in December 1995 more than 100 people were killed in flooding caused by heavy rains in KwaZulu-Natal. Most victims were from Imbali, a town near the black township of Edendale. The rains caused the Umsunduze River and its tributary to overflow. People responded in many ways to the floods. Some tried to protect their properties by blocking the doors, while others left the area. After the floods some people rebuilt their houses with whatever material was available. Others stayed away and moved to other places.

By contrast, the 1994 floods in Cape Town occurred in July. Fierce winter storms swept through the area for two weeks, affecting about 20 000 people. The South African government provided a R4 000 000 (£1 = about R8 in 1998) relief package for flood victims. The first to be helped were black residents living in a flooded area east of Cape Town in flimsy shacks of discarded cardboard, plastic and tin.

B Mean annual run-off of river systems

Drainage region	Surface area (km²)	Annual run off (million m³)	Precipitation (mm)	Run off as % of precipitation
Orange Basin	609 800	11 426	311	6.0
West Coast	75 600	937	179	0.7
South-western Cape	40 900	3 988	490	19.9
Southern Cape	87 100	1 918	304	7.2
South-eastern Cape	59 500	1 198	415	4.9
Eastern plateau slopes	152 900	21 201	845	16.4
Olifants Basin	69 200	3 201	654	7.1
Limpopo Main Basin	113 600	2 532	570	3.9
Delagoa Bay	44 700	5 533	835	14.8

Key

20 000 / 5 000 / 1 000 — Million m³ per year

------ Watersheds

C Run-off from the main drainage regions

N

0 — 300 km

LIMPOPO MAIN BASIN
OLIFANTS BASIN
Limpopo River
Crocodile River
Olifants River
DELAGOA BAY
ORANGE BASIN
Vaal River
Tugela River
Orange River
Caledon River
WEST COAST
Olifants River
SOUTH-WESTERN CAPE
Gourits River
Gamtoos River
Fish River
Kei River
EASTERN PLATEAU SLOPES
SOUTH-EASTERN CAPE
SOUTHERN CAPE

The government has also been very active in developing irrigation projects, mostly to support white **commercial farms**. By 1982 **irrigation** used up 78 per cent of all available surface water in South Africa. Government-controlled irrigation schemes account for about 450 000 hectares, about half of all irrigation in South Africa. Crops grown include citrus fruit, alfalfa and sugar.

D TWO LARGE IRRIGATION SCHEMES

The Orange River Project is the largest water development project in South Africa. It drains an area of over 412 000 km², with 13.6 per cent of South Africa's average **run-off**. It is designed to improve existing **irrigation** projects, provide more irrigation in the Lower Orange River Valley and increase flood protection. The Project will also transfer water to the Great Fish River and Sundays River using an 82 km tunnel. This will help meet industrial, domestic and hydroelectric power needs for Port Elizabeth and the Bloemfontein area.

The Lesotho Highlands Water Project is a joint venture with the mountain kingdom of Lesotho. It gives South Africa access to Lesotho's safe and abundant water resources. The Project was agreed in 1986 and a series of five dams, a power station, 240 km of tunnels and two pumping stations have been developed. This will also secure water for South Africa's

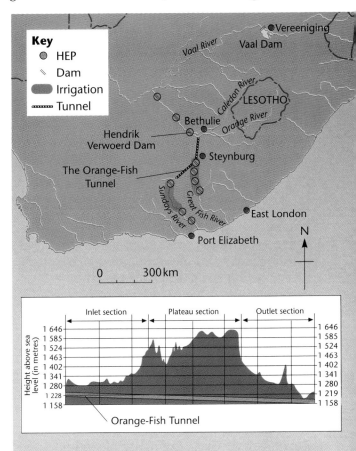

E The Orange River Project

FACT FILE

Rainfall variability

Rainfall in South Africa is unreliable and unpredictable. Large variations around the mean (average) are the rule rather than the exception. More years have below average rainfall than above average rainfall. In general the higher the rainfall, the less the variation. Hence in the north-east part of the **plateau**, Natal, the east and south coasts have least variability. By contrast, in the north-west, where it is driest, variability is greatest.

Flash floods often occur after long periods of **drought**. Notorious flash floods include those at East London (Eastern Cape) where in 1970 450 mm of rain fell in just 24 hours. Similar floods occurred at Port Elizabeth in 1968 and Natal in 1987. The highest rainfall total was recorded in 1984 at Lake St Lucia when 597 mm of rain fell in just 24 hours and was associated with the passage of the tropical cyclone Domoina.

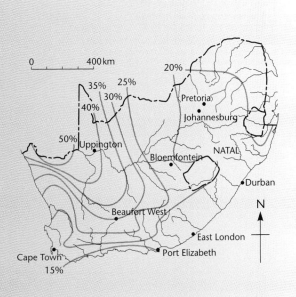

▶ What are the main environmental problems in South Africa?
▶ How have they been caused?
▶ What are the links with South Africa's history and development?

South Africa has some of the most serious environmental problems in the world. In both urban and rural areas the apartheid system was mainly to blame – in South Africa the environment is a very political problem.

Environmental problems in rural areas

In the countryside, poor farming methods have led to massive **soil erosion**, and people's need for fuel-wood has led to widespread **deforestation**. The homelands were especially at risk with thin topsoil, scarce rainfall and sloping, rocky ground. Forced resettlements caused overpopulation, leading to more **soil degradation** and deforestation. Under the conditions in which they were forced to live, people couldn't help cutting down trees, overusing soil and polluting streams.

South African farms use many **pesticides** which have been banned in Europe and the USA for many years. DDT is an example. Farm workers often have few rights and cannot read well. They use these poisons with little or no protection in a hot, windy climate.

B Industrial pollution near Cape Town

Environmental problems in urban areas

Conditions in shanty towns and squatter settlements are the most obvious signs of environmental degradation caused by apartheid. Sewage lies in puddles and rotting rubbish chokes alleys and gullies. In the torrential rains of summer this leads to regular flooding. There is limited electricity, so people burn wood or rubbish. Consequently, a cloud of smoke often covers the townships.

During the apartheid years, many oil companies refused to trade with South Africa, so coal is the main source of energy. The low wages paid to black miners keep coal prices low, but as a result coal is used wastefully, worsening pollution.

Mining industries are some of the most damaging to the environment. Mine wastes turn ground and surface waters acid, and release **toxic heavy metals**. Smelting metals releases sulphur dioxide and **toxic** air pollutants. Under apartheid, weak environmental controls helped protect South Africa's industries by keeping costs down.

A Unprotected: black workers exposed to hazardous chemicals

Disregard for black, coloured and Indian people also led to polluting industries being sited on their doorsteps. The Indian township of Merebank, near Durban, is surrounded by two oil refineries, a paper mill, a chromium processing plant and several smaller chemical factories. Merebank's children are ten times more likely to suffer from respiratory illness than children who live elsewhere.

In the 1970s, concerns about health led mining companies to close down their asbestos mines in Mafefe in the former Northern Transvaal (now Northern Province). But the companies failed to clear the mine waste. Today children play on the dangerous waste heaps between their homes and a nearby river where women fetch water.

Although attitudes towards the environment are beginning to change, it will take years for South Africa's new leaders to repair the damage apartheid has done.

C AIR POLLUTION

- 80 per cent of energy comes from coal. Each year this releases:
- one million tonnes of ash;
- one million tonnes of sulphur dioxide;
- 10 000 tonnes of iron oxide.
- Factories release a further 50 000 tonnes of sulphur dioxide a year.
- Motor vehicles release over 250 tonnes of hydrocarbons each year.

D Air pollution drifting over a black township. Notice the segmented housing and how close is it to the source of pollution

FACT FILE

Environmental demands
- Only 6 per cent of South Africa's land is protected.
  A further 4 per cent is partially protected.

There has been little change in the importance of environmental issues as a national concern since the birth of the 'new' South Africa. Such issues are likely to increase in sensitivity as South Africa's population continues to grow, and more and more resources are needed to house, feed, clothe, employ and provide health care for the rapidly growing population. Environmental issues could conflict with the demands of future economic growth.

Enviromental issues in South Africa, as indeed, most developed countries, have been seen as a preserve of the rich. This is often in stark contrast to the reality – the lives of the poor. Some of these counter-views are shown right.

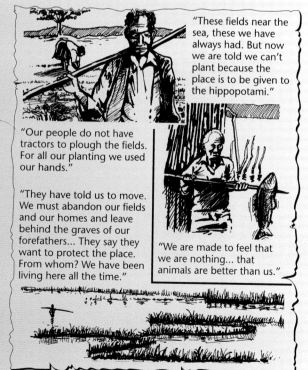

"These fields near the sea, these we have always had. But now we are told we can't plant because the place is to be given to the hippopotami."

"Our people do not have tractors to plough the fields. For all our planting we used our hands."

"They have told us to move. We must abandon our fields and our homes and leave behind the graves of our forefathers... They say they want to protect the place. From whom? We have been living here all the time."

"We are made to feel that we are nothing... that animals are better than us."

Source: M. Ramphele, *Restoring the Land*, 1991 (Panos).

> ▶ **What are drought and desertification?**
> ▶ **How do these hazards affect people, and how can they be managed?**

We have already seen that South Africa is at risk from a number of natural hazards. Some hazards such as floods are very obvious. Others such as drought and **desertification** are more long-term. These natural hazards are made worse by the actions of people, although people can also manage and control them.

Drought is a lack of water caused by high evaporation and low rainfall. About one-third of the world's land is at risk from drought. It is sometimes called a sleeping hazard because it takes a long time to take effect, perhaps over 10 years. Drought has a greater impact in drier areas because it lasts longer and there are less reserves of water. In South Africa, drought in the 1980s saw the cattle population decline by 55 per cent while maize yields dropped by 80 per cent in the 1990s.

B MAIZE PRODUCTION

In the 1970s maize yields varied between 4.2 million tonnes and 11 million tonnes. The record year for production was 1980–81 when 14.2 million tonnes were produced. Increases in maize production are due to greater use of fertilizer, high yielding varieties of maize, weed and pest control and better water conservation in the soil. South Africa needs about seven million tonnes of maize a year; the rest is exported. But during a drought there is very little surplus available for export.

Desertification is where desert features and processes gradually creep into an area due to climatic changes such as reduced rainfall. This causes vegetation to die, so more soil is exposed to erosion by wind and water.

A A dried up lake bed

But **semi-arid** climates are always unpredictable, so some geographers think desertification may not be a long-term problem.

People also cause desertification or make it worse. It is often linked to population pressure, when more people and their animals use the land. In South Africa, the early 1990s was a time of population growth and forced resettlement into semi-arid areas. This increased the demand for scarce fuel-wood for cooking, shelter, heating and fencing. In turn this led to desertification.

Little can be done to stop desertification if its causes are mainly natural. But if it is mainly caused by people then it is possible to tackle the causes. For example, on a small scale **check-dams** or **diguettes** can prevent the removal of soil from an area. On a larger scale the solution may be to reduce population pressure on small areas. Fewer animals would lead to less trampling. Planting trees might reduce wind and water erosion and provide a future source of fuel.

D Gulley erosion caused by overgrazing

	1990/1	1991/2	1992/3
Dry beans	100	27	61
Grain sorghum	240	98	380
Groundnuts	78	80	119
Soya beans	126	68	60
Sunflower seeds	589	174	364
White maize	3180	1232	4351
Yellow maize	4016	1690	4542

C Summer crop production (1 000 tonnes), 1990/1–1992/3

E Diguettes (check-dams) used to prevent soil erosion

FACT FILE

Elements of desertification
Four elements have been identified in the process of desertification. These are sometimes called 'the 4 Ds'.

- **drylands** – 'susceptible to experiencing full desert conditions if mismanaged' – this is a climatic definition that implies fragility

- **drought** – two or more years with rainfall substantially below the mean average

- **degradation** – 'a reduction or destruction of the biological potential' – this is usually associated with unsound human practises such as **overgrazing**, **deforestation**, trampling, and overproduction

- **desertification** – the combination of human and climatic variables which leads to the irreversible decline of the land.

Desertification and soil erosion in the Eastern Cape

▶ **What are the causes of desertification and soil erosion in the Eastern Cape?**
▶ **What is being done about it?**

Ciskei is one of South Africa's former homelands, now part of the Eastern Cape. It only covers a small area (7760 km^2), but has great contrasts in relief, climate and vegetation. It has four main regions (**A**) but only the Amatola Basin is much use for agriculture.

Rainfall comes mostly in summer storms, with over 70 per cent between October and November. On the coast rainfall is more even throughout the year, but in the north it is low and irregular. Drought in the late 1970s and 1980s made farming even more difficult here. In the north, temperature ranges are greater and there is a greater risk of frost, so the growing season is shorter.

Soils in most of the area are not good enough for farming without irrigation. Most of the area has **bushveld** vegetation which is only suitable for browsing animals like goats. Only one-tenth is any good for grazing by animals like cows.

Land degradation is common in South Africa's former homelands like Ciskei. Up to 46 per cent of the land was moderately or severely eroded, and 39 per cent of its pastures **overgrazed**. Half of Ciskei's surface was more or less eroded and only 23 per cent was intact. Erosion **gullies** now look like small valleys, many 20 metres deep.

Thornhill was a 'temporary' resettlement camp, one of the many parched, desperately poor communities in the homelands which were artificially created under apartheid. The 660 000 population doubled between 1950 and 1980 – one quarter was forcibly relocated here in the 1970s. It is a harsh environment, with thousands of brown mud houses and rusty shacks scattered over dry, loose soil. But the land cannot sustain the people who live there and there is little sanitation and water.

Extreme poverty is often closely linked with environmental disasters. With hardly any job opportunities, it is vital for people to plant some crops and raise some livestock. However, because there is not enough land to go round, pressure on natural resources increases each year.

In Ciskei, more than half the farms in the best grazing areas are overstocked with cattle, by up to 77 per cent. Each household uses three to four tonnes of fuel-wood a year. In this fragile environment the vegetation never recovers and dustbowl conditions are created.

Soil erosion has also affected water supplies. Many springs have dried up since the 1970s, so much of Ciskei's water is now brought in by lorry. Erosion means the soil absorbs less rainfall, so more runs off the surface. This causes a downward spiral of environmental and economic crisis. The result is the migration of people from the land to the fringes of urban areas.

Unfortunately little is being done to improve the environment. The government has little money to tackle the problems. Locally, many young people who could help change things have left, leaving behind an ageing population.

A LAND USE IN CISKEI

Recommended amount of land for each sheep or goat: 0.85 hectare

Actual amount of land per animal: 0.04 hectare

	1946	1981
Average size of land holding	1.72 ha.	0.43 ha.
Landless people	10%	43%

B THE IMPACT ON LOCALS

The low rainfall over the past decade devastated agriculture in the area, one resident recalled.

"my three cattle died ... we had nothing to plough the land ... we had to wait for the government tractors ... we had to wait a long time ... and then the rains did not to come."

C Dried up soil – the effect of drought

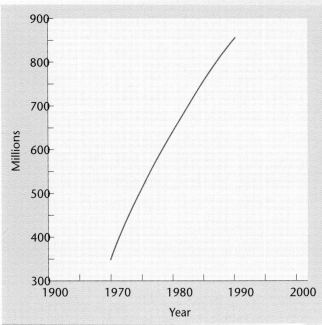

E Population growth in the Eastern Cape, 1970–85

D Even in more watered, fertile areas, overgrazing causes severe soil erosion

FACT FILE

Soil erosion in the Eastern Cape
The increase in soil erosion is due to a number of factors:
- climatic change (a more variable/seasonal rainfall)
- vegetation removal (due to increased population pressure)
- cultivation of marginal lands (dry areas)
- intensification of agriculture
- heavier and more powerful machinery
- compaction of soil
- cultivation of steeper slopes
- field enlargement
- hedgerow removal
- planting of winter cereals.

The impact of soil erosion also includes:
- declining **productivity**
- decreasing organic and moisture content
- increased turbidity (murkiness) in streams.

South Africa's population

▶ **What is the make-up of the population?**
▶ **Where do people live?**
▶ **How fast is population growth?**

A multicultural population

South Africa's population is about 40 million, made up of four main groups (**A, B**). South Africa's black population are the people who lived in South Africa long before the first white **colony** was set up at the Cape in 1652. There are about 31 million black people from different tribal groups such as the Zulus and the Xhosa. Tribes originally came from different places but they now live in all parts of the country, especially in the urban-industrial areas.

The five million white people are mostly descended from English and Dutch **colonists**, as well as German, Italian and Portuguese settlers. The Afrikaner people are descended from Dutch settlers; they have their own language. There are about one million Asians who mainly live in urban areas. Finally there are also some three million people from mixed backgrounds, who were called coloured under the apartheid system.

One important difference between this **population composition** is its growth and structure, which we investigate here and on pages 24–25. Another is quality of life, which we investigate on pages 26–27.

A South Africa's youthful population

	1970	**1995**
Black	70.5%	76.3%
White	17.0%	12.7%
Coloured	9.6%	8.5%
Asian	2.9%	2.5%
Total (millions)	22 707	41 244

B Changes in the make-up of South Africa's population, 1970–95

Population growth

South Africa's population is growing at a rate of about 2.4% a year. Growth rates are so high that by the year 2010 South Africa's population could be between 50 and 60 million (**C**). The population is growing because more people are being born than are dying. Better health means people's **life expectancy** is increasing, and **infant mortality** is declining. However, these figures hide big inequalities between black and white people (**E**).

Population growth varies for different groups. Black people have the highest growth rates, nearly 3 per cent a year, because of their youthful population. Population growth also varies across the country. Between 1948 and 1990 the most rapid growth was in the black townships and the homelands. A fast-growing population puts pressure on the environment and resources, as well as on services like education and health.

Population distribution

The distribution of South Africa's population is very uneven (**D**). There are high **population densities** where resources, industry and services attract people and help them to make a living. Examples are urban-industrial areas such as Gauteng, around major cities such as Durban and rural areas with good opportunities for farming.

In general, population decreases from the south-east to north-west. This partly reflects the distribution of rainfall in South Africa: the lowest densities are found in the most arid areas and also in parts of the mountains. Population distribution is also changing; after the end of apartheid, thousands of people left the homelands and migrated to large cities in search of employment (see pages 28–29).

	1960	1990	1994
Life expectancy:			
Men	55.7 years	60.7 years	60 years
Women	59.7 years	66.3 years	75 years
Infant Mortality (per 1000 births)	80	62	53
Fertility (average number of children a woman has)	6	4.6	4

E Changes in life expectancy, infant mortality and fertility in South Africa

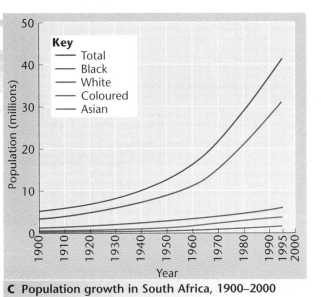

C Population growth in South Africa, 1900–2000

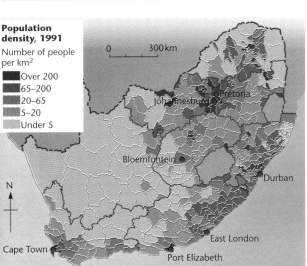

D Population density in South Africa, 1991

FACT FILE

South Africa's population

South Africa's main racial groups 1998 estimate

	Million	**%**
Black	31.5	76
White	5.4	13
Asian	1.2	3
Coloured	3.3	8
Total	41.4	100

Racial diversity is reflected by a diversity in languages. South Africa has 11 official languages!

Official language	**Share of population (%)**
Zulu	22.4
Xhosa	18.3
Afrikaans	14.5
Pedi	9.1
English	8.4
Setswana	7.7
Sesotho	6.4
Tsonga	3.7
Siswati	3.1
Venda	1.7
Ndebele	0.7
Other languages	4.0

▶ Why is the population growing so fast?

Populations change due to:
- changes in the **birth rate** – the number of children born;
- changes in the **death rate** – the number of people dying;
- migration – people moving in or out the country.

The difference between the birth and death rates is called the rate of **natural increase**. Because the birth rate in South Africa is much higher than the death rate, the population is growing fast. The balance of birth and death rates is a good sign of a country's development, because they are linked with people's health, wealth and education. In South Africa, the differences between black and white people clearly show the inequalities brought about under apartheid.

The birth rate
What causes high birth rates? People want children:
- to help out and earn money;
- to look after them in old age;
- to replace other children who have died (**B**);
- to continue the family name;
- for status.

B Among black people, the IMR is still very high – partly as a result the birth rate is high

Birth rates come down when:
- women are well educated;
- women can make choices about their lives and work;
- the government looks after people through pensions and health services;
- family planning services are available;
- infant mortality is low – there is less need for replacing children;
- children are expensive to bring up.

The death rate
Why are death rates high?
- lack of clean water, poor hygiene and sanitation;
- lack of food;
- overcrowding and disease;
- poverty.

Death rates come down when there is:
- clean water, good hygiene and sanitation;
- a reliable food supply;
- lower population densities;
- better health care;
- rising standards of living

	1970	1980	1990
Black*			
Birth rate	40.0	40.0	35.0
Death rate	12.0	12.0	12.0
White			
Birth rate	22.9	16.5	13.8
Death rate	8.9	8.3	6.6
Coloured			
Birth rate	34.1	27.1	23.8
Death rate	13.3	8.8	7.6
Asian			
Birth rate	32.3	24.1	20.6
Death rate	6.7	5.9	4.3

* estimates

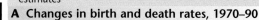

A Changes in birth and death rates, 1970–90

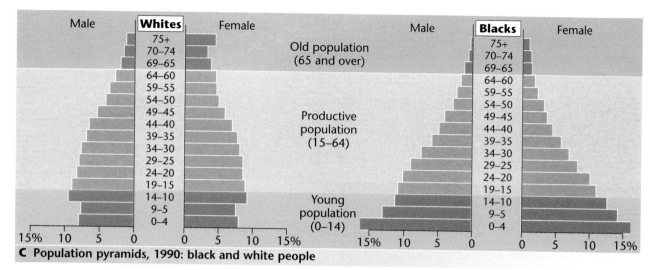

C Population pyramids, 1990: black and white people

Age	0–4	5–9	10–14	15–19	20–24	25–29	30–34	35–39	40–44	45–49	50–54	55–59	60–64	65–69	70–74	75+
Male %	10.0	10.5	11.5	10.5	10.0	9.0	8.5	8.0	5.5	5.0	4.0	3.0	2.0	1.5	1.0	1.0
Female %	10.0	10.5	11.5	10.5	10.0	9.0	8.5	8.0	5.5	5.0	3.5	2.5	2.0	2.0	0.5	2.0

D Population structure: Asian people

Population structure

Population pyramids show the balance between males and females and the balance between different age groups (**C**). In South Africa, population pyramids also show the inequalities between different groups. The pyramid for black people shows a high proportion of children because birth rates are high. The pyramid for white people has fewer children and more old people, because of a longer life expectancy and low birth rate.

FACT FILE

The Demographic Transition Model (DTM)
The DTM describes how birth rates and death rates change over time. It is divided into four stages (and sometimes a fifth).
Stage 1 Early expanding
- Birth rates and death rates are high and variable
- population growth fluctuates
- there are no countries now at this stage although some indigenous (primitive) tribes are
- the UK was at this stage until about 1750.
Stage 2 Early expanding
- The birth rate remains high but the death rate comes down rapidly
- population growth is rapid
- countries such as Afghanistan, Sudan and Libya are at this stage
- the UK passed through this stage by 1850.

Stage 3 Late expanding
- The birth rate drops and the death rate remains low
- population growth continues but at a smaller rate
- Brazil and Argentina are at this stage
- the UK passed through this stage in about 1950.
Stage 4 Low and variable
- Birth rates and death rates are low and variable
- population growth fluctuates
- the UK and most developed countries are now at this stage.
Stage 5 Low and declining
- The birth rate is lower than the death rate
- the population declines.

▶ What is the Human Development Index?
▶ How does it vary in South Africa?

A Many black South Africans have a very low standard of living.

B Inside municipal (council) housing, Dimbaza, Eastern Cape

The Human Development Index (HDI) is used by the United Nations to measure human development. It includes three measures of a decent life:

• Life expectancy;
• Knowledge (**adult literacy** and average number of years in school);
• Standard of living, adjusted to the local cost of living.

The Human Development Index (HDI) can help show differences between countries: in general, richer countries with a high **Gross National Product (GNP)** also have a high HDI (**C**). But these national averages can hide differences within a country, for example between black and white people in South Africa.

Map **D** shows variations between South Africa's regions. South Africa's least developed areas are the former homelands, where most people are poorly-paid farm workers. By contrast, high HDIs are found near major cities, on the KwaZulu-Natal coastline and along parts of the Garden Route, the coastal area between Cape Town and George. These are rich, fertile areas which attract wealthy people as well as creating productive agriculture.

Rank	Country	HDI rating	GNP($ US) per person (1994)
1	Canada	0.932	20,520
16	UK	0.911	17,160
23	Spain	0.888	13,400
	White South Africans	0.878	N/A
24	Hong Kong	0.875	20,340
54	Thailand	0.798	8,950
93	South Africa	0.650	3,799
94	China	0.644	1,950
122	Cape Verde	0.474	1,750
	Black South Africans	0.462	N/A
123	Congo	0.461	2,870
173	Guinea	0.191	592

C HDI rating for selected countries, 1994

South Africa has huge inequalities in wealth and standard of living (C). Up to 16 million people live below the **Minimum Living Level**. This includes 33 per cent of black households in urban areas, and 80 per cent in rural areas (D). By contrast, 38 per cent of white people earn between R10 000 and R29 999.

Infant mortality rate

The **Infant Mortality Rate (IMR)** shows the number of children who die before their first birthday, out of every 1 000 born. It is a good indicator of a nation's development, because babies' health is affected by water supply, sanitation, housing, food supply and income levels. The lower the IMR the more developed the country. In South Africa, IMR rates are coming down as the country develops. But there are big differences in infant mortality between rural areas (higher) urban areas (lower), and between different groups (E).

FACT FILE

The Infant Mortality Rate
In South Africa reliable statistics relating to the IMR are scarce, although it is possible to see the main trends.
- First, it varies with race, whites having lower rates (c. 10–15 per cent), than blacks (c. 50–100 per cent), although the rates for both are decreasing. The latest data suggest rates per thousand of over 52 for blacks, 28 for coloureds, 13.5 for Indians and 7.3 for whites.
- The IMR also varies spatially, being higher in the **peri-urban** and **rural** areas compared with urban areas. Nevertheless, there is considerable variation between cities, as well as within cities, ranging from 12 per cent in Durban to 41.3 per cent in Port Elizabeth.

Cause and time of death among infants also varies
- For whites, **neonatal** and **perinatal** deaths were more likely, due to congenital deformities
- By contrast black deaths are more likely to be due to low birth-weight, gastro-enteritis, pneumonia and jaundice, occurring between 7–365 days, the post-neonatal period.

D Human development, 1993

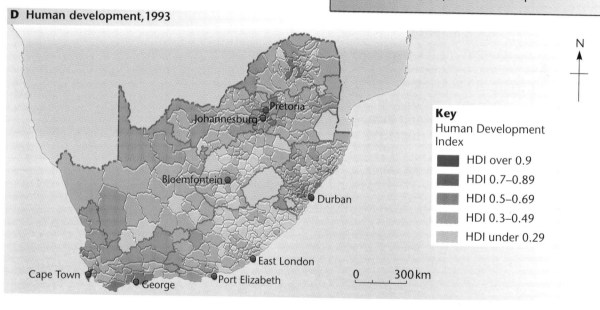

Key
Human Development Index
- HDI over 0.9
- HDI 0.7–0.89
- HDI 0.5–0.69
- HDI 0.3–0.49
- HDI under 0.29

	Black	White	Coloured	Indian
Infant Mortality Rate (per 1 000 live births)	52.8	7.3	28.0	3.5
Life expectancy (years)	63	73	63	67
TB cases per 100 000 people	216	15	580	53
School expenditure per head (rand)	1 248	4 448	2 701	3 500
School pass rate (%)	41	96	83	95
Average monthly income (rand)	779	4 679	1 607	2 476

E Social and economic indicators in South Africa, 1993

> ▶ What is migration?
> ▶ What types of migration have occurred in South Africa?

Migration is the movement of people from one place to another. It is a permanent change in the place a person lives. Migration generally occurs over a long distance, rather than small-scale movements within a town or city. Migration can be forced or voluntary.

South Africa has had three main periods of migration in the twentieth century:
• economic migration linked with industrial development until 1950;
• forced migration related to apartheid;
• voluntary migration following the collapse of the apartheid system.

Industry in South Africa developed rapidly between the two world wars. Many black people migrated from the countryside to cities to work in the growing gold and diamond mines. They were known as **migrant labourers**. As the population grew in the cities there was increased demand for food products. Agricultural Marketing Boards guaranteed farmers a fixed price for their goods – this made farming quite profitable, and many farmers evicted black tenants from their land. Many of these drifted back to the **reserves** (early forms of homelands) or the townships (**A**).

Between 1948 and 1994 the white National Party had political control of South Africa and set up the apartheid policy. Under this policy, over four million black people were forcibly removed from 'white' areas and relocated to the homelands. At the same time, there were severe restrictions on black people entering 'white' towns – these restrictions were known as **influx control**. So industries and farms owned by white people were able to recruit black workers from the homelands (**B**).

Since the end of apartheid many black people have migrated from the homelands in search of work in large cities. However, because of their poverty, they are forced to live in the townships on the edge of cities. So although apartheid is officially over, for many people discrimination is still widespread due to their poverty.

There is also much migration among the white population. In the first part of this century many white people were **immigrants** from Europe. Since 1990, over 250 000 white people have **emigrated** from South Africa. Also, a small number of Afrikaners have left South Africa and set up farms in neighbouring countries.

A Migration in South Africa, 1935–50

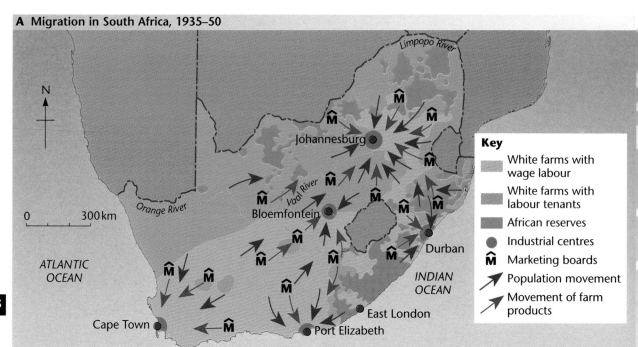

Key
- White farms with wage labour
- White farms with labour tenants
- African reserves
- Industrial centres
- M̂ Marketing boards
- Population movement
- Movement of farm products

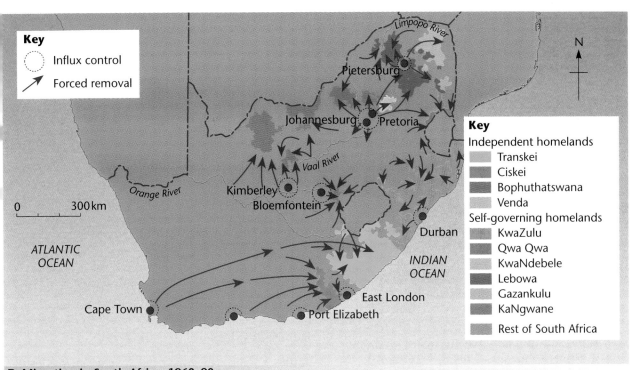

B Migration in South Africa, 1960–90

Key
◯ Influx control
↗ Forced removal

Key
Independent homelands
  Transkei
  Ciskei
  Bophuthatswana
  Venda
Self-governing homelands
  KwaZulu
  Qwa Qwa
  KwaNdebele
  Lebowa
  Gazankulu
  KaNgwane

  Rest of South Africa

C FORCED REMOVALS TO DIMBAZA, CISKEI

'Dimbaza is a dumping ground for the unwanted and non-productive population. They were dumped in isolated settlements lacking all services. They were the poorest, the least skilled, the least organized groups of people in South Africa.'

Local priest

'In Uppingham we thought we were third class citizens. When we were driven to Dimbaza we realized we were not citizens at all and we didn't have any class either. We were moved about just like cattle being taken to market.'

A resident removed to Dimbaza

FACT FILE

Migration
There has been a long history of migration in South Africa as the map shows.

Key
 Black Africans whose language is from the Bantu family of languages (300–AD1000)

The Zulu Mfecane or Difagane (scattering of peoples) resulting from the expansion of the Zulu Empire (1820s and 1830s)

TSWANA Former African chiefdoms (the names do not show their whole territory or twentieth- century language area)

SAN The first human inhabitants of South Africa

Europeans

Afrikaner (Boer) settlers Great Trek (1835–42) who migrated to escape from British rule in the Cape

Indians arrived from 1860 to work on sugar plantations

Slaves imported by the Dutch from their colonies in the East Indies (seventeenth and eighteenth centuries)

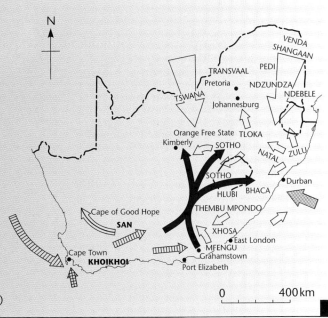

Urbanization and inequality

▶ **What was the apartheid city?**
▶ **How is it changing?**

Urbanization

South Africa's urban areas are increasing at an alarming rate. In 1990, 63 per cent of South Africa's population were **urbanized**, ranging from 89 per cent among white, coloured and Indian people to 50 per cent among black people. By 2000, 33 million people (75 per cent) will be urban.

Now that the restrictions of apartheid have been removed, black **urbanization** is rising rapidly. Up to fourteen million more black people will live in urban areas over the next two decades. How will this affect the **post-apartheid city** in South Africa?

A An aerial view of Kayelitsha township, Cape Town

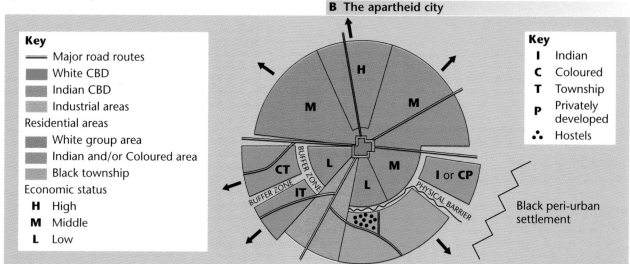

B The apartheid city

Key
━━ Major road routes
⬛ White CBD
⬛ Indian CBD
⬛ Industrial areas
Residential areas
⬛ White group area
⬛ Indian and/or Coloured area
⬛ Black township
Economic status
H High
M Middle
L Low

Key
I Indian
C Coloured
T Township
P Privately developed
∴ Hostels

Black peri-urban settlement

The 'apartheid city'

Cities in South Africa were planned with a special layout (**B**). In the centre was the Central Business District (CBD) dominated by white people. This CBD was surrounded by white residential areas. Coloured, Indian and black townships were separated from the white areas by physical barriers, parks, or industrial zones.

The post-apartheid city

After apartheid, one change has been that groups are not segregated into different areas by law. But the biggest problem is the speed of urbanization.

C Destroying the signs of apartheid?

The urban population is growing rapidly as a result of migration and natural increase, especially in the squatter settlements. There are serious problems in providing even the basic necessities of life, such as water and sanitation, let alone healthcare, education and employment.

But in future the structure of cities is unlikely to change much unless resources, wealth and opportunities are shared more equally. Few black people will be able to afford houses in the former white areas, especially the more expensive areas. Most white people will not want to live in the townships.

Many black people will still live in squatter shacks in the sprawling peri-urban townships, without adequate water, sanitation or jobs. Most people with jobs will continue to face long and expensive journeys to work in the city.

The housing crisis

South Africa faces some of the worst housing problems in the world and the backlog of over one million houses is rising rapidly. New housing generally favours whites. In 1991 only one-quarter of new houses were built at a cost of less than R65 000, so new houses are built for the wealthy, more of whom are white. Since most black people earn less than R2 000 a month, their chance of buying a new home is limited.

Improving housing is a top priority for the new government but there is a severe shortage of funds. It favours the idea of building starter homes: a core foundation, one room and basic services at a cost of about R20 000. These can be upgraded when the occupant can afford it.

E Poor quality housing in Peelton, Eastern Cape

F Informal (squatter) housing in Zwelitsha, Eastern Cape

D THE HOUSING CRISIS

- 13 million people have no proper home
- 4.4 million households but only 3.4 million homes
- 4.5 million 'informal' houses
- 35 per cent of informal houses are in cities, 65 per cent in rural areas
- 33 per cent of the rural population live in decent homes
- Average floor area: 33m² per white person, 4m² per black person

FACT FILE

Urban inequality
Source: *The Guardian,* April 11 1998
'Fly into any South African city and the divisions are precise and entrenched. Johannesburg offers the most vivid example. On one side, there is Sandton municipality, where, in fortified splendour, live some of the most pampered people on Earth. They do not all live in 'Italianate' palaces, with decorative fountains rising out of decorative lawns.

... But white enclaves, such as Sandton, are apartheid's unchallenged bastions, from which 5 per cent of the population control 88 per cent of the nation's wealth. This grotesque imbalance of power has not changed since democracy.'

Rural settlement

▶ **What are rural areas like?**
▶ **What pressures do black people in rural areas face?**
▶ **How do people and the environment affect each other?**

In rural areas, only 33 per cent of the population have decent quality houses. Up to ten million people live in informal houses, sub-standard huts and shacks, made of any available materials. These houses are often overcrowded, with up to eleven people per house in places, with little access to facilities like water, sanitation and electricity.

Welcomewood is a rural area in the Eastern Cape and Border region of South Africa. Parts of the area were originally used for commercial farming but much of the land is too hilly and steep for farming. The village of Welcomewood was developed in order to house black people displaced by the apartheid system. It is a village of about 2 000 people with a primary school, clinic and two water taps.

A The main road in Welcomewood showing a creche (white building) and looking east towards the school and the clinic

B Looking south from Welcomewood towards the Indian Ocean, showing vegetation, slopes and landforms

FACT FILE

Maps and orthophotos
Maps tell us a great deal about the landscape and the activities that take place in an area. If we use photographs as well we get a very strong feeling for what a place is like – even if that place is a long way from home. Geographers use many tools in their attempts to understand about people and places. Here we have used three methods, OS maps, orthophotos and ordinary photos to get a feel for a place which is many thousands of miles away and whose people speak another language. But through our study we can begin to understand the area in which they live.

An orthophoto is an aerial photograph with contour lines on. It gives us a visual impression of an area and also provides us with some hard facts, or data, about the **relief** of an area. They are often used in remote areas where it is easier to send planes with photographers over, rather than sending in engineers on the ground. They are a quick and efficient way of learning about an area.

In remote areas, as well as rapidly changing areas – such as **townships** – the use of aerial photographs and satellites are essential for geographers to map an area and assess levels of change. As population censuses occur only every ten years or so – aerial photos (and orthophotos) are a great help to estimate the physical and human geography of an area.

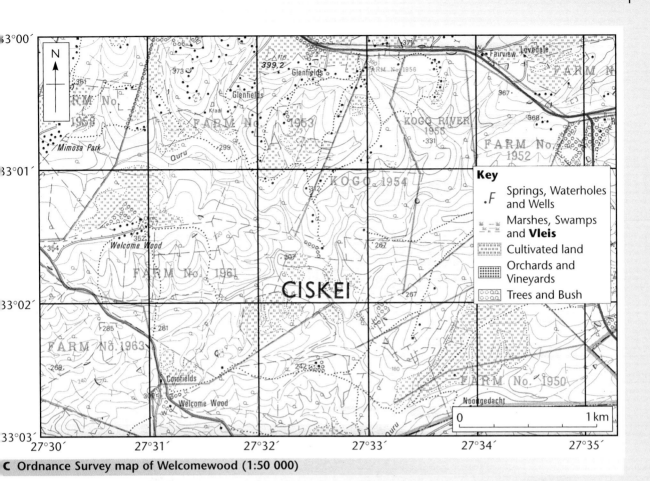

C Ordnance Survey map of Welcomewood (1:50 000)

Key

.F Springs, Waterholes and Wells

Marshes, Swamps and **Vleis**

Cultivated land

Orchards and Vineyards

Trees and Bush

D An orthophoto (an aerial photograph with contour lines) showing Welcomewood

A black township, Fingo Village, Grahamstown

▶ What is it like to live in Fingo Village?
▶ How have population changes and inequality affected this area?

A Fingo Village, Grahamstown

B Low environmental quality, Fingo Village, Grahamstown

- low household incomes, most less than R500 per month;
- many people have to travel long distances to work, often two to three hours each day;
- many of the very poor people spend up to 70 per cent of their income on food, 10 per cent on fuel and up to 10 per cent on rent and transport. They have very little money to spend on luxuries.

There are also many related social problems:
- over 50 per cent of the population is under 18 years old;
- large households, on average over six people per household;
- rapid population growth, up to 4 per cent per year;
- many illnesses such as TB, measles, diarrhoea and vomiting;
- very high rates of crime;
- lack of proper schools and health care.

There are also many environmental problems:
- poor quality housing without services such as electricity, sanitation and running water;
- poor roads and communications;
- air, water and soil pollution are widespread and increasing.

Fingo Village is a black township on the outskirts of Grahamstown in the Eastern Cape. Conditions in the whole of this region are poor, but they are very harsh in some townships like Grahamstown. There are a number of economic, social and environmental problems.

Economic problems include:
- 34 per cent unemployment;
- 28 per cent underemployment (people who have jobs but would like to work for longer hours);
- high rents for housing;
- low wages (average weekly wages are R100);

C A FINGO VILLAGE RESIDENT, WHO WORKS AT RHODES UNIVERSITY

'In some ways we are lucky. There are jobs at Rhodes University although they are not very well paid. Our houses are OK – but compared with the ones in parts of Grahamstown such as Cross Street they are small, overcrowded and lacking in facilities. We could be worse off – we certainly could be better off. Personally I get very tired having to walk up the hill to Rhodes each day. But at least it's a job – it means I can support my family. I wish that Fingo Village had more play areas, a sports ground for instance. Perhaps Nelson Mandela will be able to sort it ...'

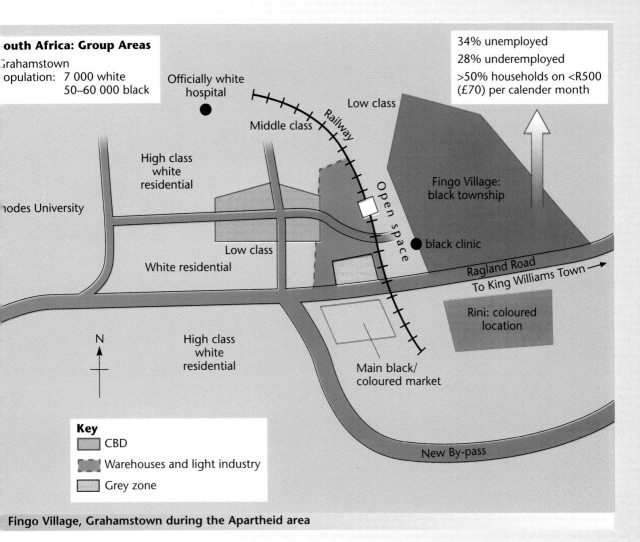

South Africa: Group Areas

Grahamstown
population: 7 000 white
50–60 000 black

Officially white hospital

Low class

Middle class

Railway

High class white residential

Rhodes University

Open space

Fingo Village: black township

black clinic

Low class
White residential

Ragland Road
To King Williams Town →

34% unemployed
28% underemployed
>50% households on <R500 (£70) per calender month

N

High class white residential

Rini: coloured location

Main black/ coloured market

New By-pass

Key
CBD
Warehouses and light industry
Grey zone

Fingo Village, Grahamstown during the Apartheid area

FACT FILE

Housing inequality

Housing inequality is the most concrete illustration of the legacy of **apartheid**. Whereas most white South Africans live in adequately serviced and comfortable housing, the majority of black South Africans live in overcrowded dwellings that often lack basic services.

Countrywide about 13 million people do not have proper homes.

In 1990 it was estimated that 60 per cent of the 1.8 million African people resident in the Durban area lived in shacks, and in Gauteng half of the African population, some 2.6 million people, resided in backyard or free-standing shacks. 1.7 million – 70 per cent – of South African

households earn less than 1500 Rand ($375) a month and thus do not have the financial means to acquire a home of their own.

The backlog of housing is one of many problems that the South African government is having to face. There are related problems of education, health, welfare and economic development. The government would like private companies to provide housing – rather than the government paying for them all. However, private companies want to make a profit – so they build houses for the rich – not for the poor. Hence there is a lack of affordable housing in South Africa (There is a similar problem in many British cities – such as Oxford and Manchester).

4 ECONOMIC ENVIRONMENTS

The two sides of South African agriculture

▶ **What types of farming are found in South Africa?**
▶ **What are the differences between black and white farmers?**
▶ **What problems do farmers face?**

South Africa's agriculture shows the two sides of the country's economy. The contrasts between the mainly white commercial farms and the mainly black **subsistence farms** could hardly be greater. **Commercial farms** produce 90 per cent of the income from farming, but most jobs are in subsistence black farming.

In some ways farming is a success story. In normal years South Africa produces good food surpluses, and 30 per cent of exports apart from gold come from agricultural products. South Africa produces:
- more than 50 per cent of the food for Southern Africa;
- 45 per cent of Africa's maize and wool production;
- 27 per cent of Africa's wheat;
- 20 per cent of Africa's potatoes;
- 17 per cent of Africa's red meat.

Commercial agriculture
Commercial agriculture in South Africa is dominated by white farmers, although their numbers are decreasing. For example in the 1950s there were more than 100 000 commercial farmers but by 1995 only 65 000. The development of commercial agriculture has been based on exploiting the black labour force.

Farming in the former homelands
Although the black 'homelands' no longer exist, little has changed there. Partly due to the variety of the natural environments, black agriculture varies greatly too. In 1955 a Government report found that the homeland areas had up to 50 per cent more good farmland

than areas in white South Africa. However, this did not take into account the problems of **accessibility** and **population pressure**.

The problems of black subsistence agriculture are linked to a shortage of land, a growing population and increasing poverty. These lead to:
- overcrowding;
- overgrazing;
- use of poor land;
- soil erosion;
- declining yields.

A White commercial farming

B Black subsistence farming in South Africa

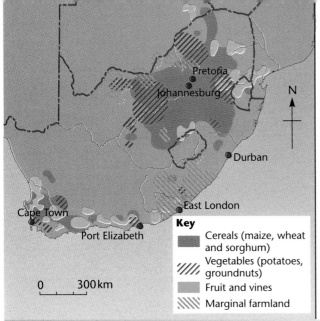
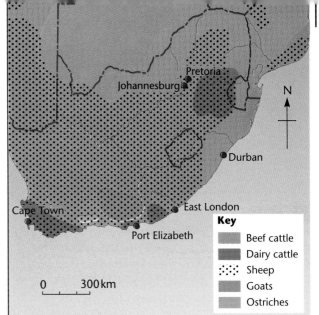

Key

▨	Cereals (maize, wheat and sorghum)
▥	Vegetables (potatoes, groundnuts)
▨	Fruit and vines
▨	Marginal farmland

0 — 300 km

Key

▨	Beef cattle
▨	Dairy cattle
⁙	Sheep
▨	Goats
▨	Ostriches

0 — 300 km

C Commercial agriculture in South Africa

	Homeland area (largely black)	Non-homeland area (largely white)	Total
Total area (million ha)	17.3	102.3	119.6
Farmland (ha)	16.1	83.1	99.2
Rural population (million)	13.1	5.3	18.4
Farmland per person (ha)	0.2	15.7	5.4
Average farm size (ha)	1	1 300	

	Homeland area (largely black)	Non-homeland area (largely white)
Share of marketed production	4%	96%
Average productivity per person per year	R2/ha	R11/ha
Share of agricultural GDP	10%	90%

D Inequalities in South African farming, 1990

FACT FILE

Black agriculture

Working conditions for blacks vary greatly. For most, wages are very low and there is limited security. Wages are frequently only about 10 per cent of manufacturing wages although **payment in kind** sometimes doubled their income. At one extreme there are farms where flogging, child labour, and payment by the 'tot' system, namely part payment in the form of alcohol, is common. Weekly wages can be as low as R35 for women and R45 for men (R7 = 1 English Pound). At the other extreme, some farmers provide their labourers with three-bedroomed houses, creche facilities, a school and a library. Wages of up to R125 per week were reported.

Some of the best farmland in South Africa is in homeland areas, namely KwaZulu and Transkei. By contrast it also has some of the worst, such as in Ciskei. In a recent survey of homeland areas,

	1970	1980	1990	2000	2020
Cultivated	0.6	0.5	0.4	0.3	0.2
Other	5.5	4.2	3.2	2.4	1.5

E Land per person in South Africa, 1970–2020

31 per cent of rural households were living below subsistence levels, 13 per cent of rural households farmed on a small scale and only 0.2 per cent of farmers farmed on a commercial basis.

Total food production in the homeland areas is sufficient for about one third of the homeland needs. The failure to modernise and to increase output is related to a number of factors:
- the limited size of plots
- yields up to five times less than on white farms
- up to 20 to 30 per cent of the land is left unused.

▶ Why is South Africa an important industrial country?
▶ What problems face big business?
▶ What is the informal economy?

South Africa's resources

The South African economy is the largest in the whole of the African continent, although its future is very uncertain. South Africa's strength lies in its resources (table A). In human resources, South Africa has a large established workforce and an **infrastructure** (factories, mines, roads, transport networks) built up over many years of industrial growth.

Manganese	79%
Platinum	70%
Chrome	55%
Gold	48%
Alumino-silicates	38%
Vanadium	33%

A South Africa's share of some of the world's mineral resources

Jobs and incomes

About one-third of the population is in employment, most in manufacturing industry (19 per cent) and government (17 per cent). In most jobs, differences in wages between black and white workers have declined over the last twenty years, but there is still a big difference in overall incomes (table **D**).

The **formal economy** does not provide enough job opportunities for the majority of the population, but there is a vibrant **informal economy**. This includes a variety of jobs such as domestic work, gardening and selling food, taxi driving and running **shebeens** (illegal drinking parlours). Black businesses are held back by problems such as a lack of credit from banks; poor training and skills; violence, theft and instability in townships; and competition from white business and from overseas.

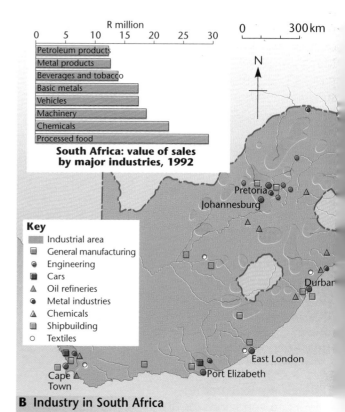

South Africa: value of sales by major industries, 1992

Key
- Industrial area
- General manufacturing
- Engineering
- Cars
- Oil refineries
- Metal industries
- Chemicals
- Shipbuilding
- Textiles

B Industry in South Africa

	Agriculture	Industry	Services
1970	21%	22%	57%
1994	13%	25%	62%

C Changes in the economy: jobs

Monthly household income, 1993	
Black	R662
Coloured	R1279
Indian	R2005
White	R3931

Share of personal income, 1993		
	% of population	Share of income
Black	74%	33%
White	14%	54%

D Income, 1993

E M HOLMAN QUOTING THE MONITOR COMPANY IN THE FINANCIAL TIMES, 2 MAY 1995

'We must not be fooled by the new factories, offices and shopping malls into thinking that the underlying industries are globally competitive. Underneath the attractively painted body panels, the engine is rusty and out-dated.'

South Africa's problems

South Africa's economy is uncompetitive. For example, it costs more to transport steel from the centre of South Africa to Durban than it does to transport it from Durban to Europe! Many South African industries survived in the past only because of state protection and subsidies. Today some companies serve very small markets, and so have high costs. Although workers in South Africa are cheap, their **productivity** is very low. South Africa is not as rich as it seems: **Gross Domestic Product (GDP)** (the wealth a country produces) per person is similar to Brazil or Botswana.

A major problem facing the new government is that economic growth is only 1 per cent a year, while population growth is 3 per cent. Since 1991 new investment has been limited. The reasons include uncertainty about South African's future, continuing violence, high rates of inflation, and increased competition from other developing countries.

FACT FILE

The need for economic changes
South Africa needs an economic transformation just as far reaching as that achieved in the political arena. The Government of National Unity has to reach growth rates comparable to the Asian **NICs** if it is to redress the legacy of **apartheid**.

South Africa needs higher productivity, more flexible labour markets and more efficient management if it is to become internationally competitive. Although it has received overseas investment, many investors are reluctant to invest too much.

One area of growth has been in the taxi sector. This has developed into a powerful feature of the urban informal economy. The 10- to 15-seater minibus taxis are faster and more flexible than buses and trains, so they are very popular. However they are often overcrowded and charge high fares, and as they are often driven recklessly, accidents are frequent. Despite this, the staggering growth of taxis has been an important part of small business development by black people in South Africa.

F **South Africa's black taxis: one of the most vibrant parts of the ecomomy**

South Africa is uncompetitive. The following figures show labour costs and manpower hours to construct a car in South Africa, Mexico and the USA.

	Labour costs per hour	Labour hours per car	Labour costs per car (US$)
South Africa	5.6	64	358.4
Mexico	6.0	24	144.0
USA	38.0	19	722.0

▶ **Why is gold so important in South Africa?**
▶ **What effects is the decline of gold having on people and the economy?**

Gold has been an important part of the economy since the 1880s. Gold allowed South Africa to change from an economy based mainly on agriculture to one based on mining. Some of the profits from gold and diamond mining were invested in manufacturing industries; this broadened and strengthened the economy.

Gold is an important **resource** and **raw material** (C). However, the future of gold mining is not healthy and production is falling (A).

Problems in gold mining

There are two main problems.

- The world price of gold is falling, reaching a twelve-year low in 1997. At this price, more than half of South Africa's gold mines are unprofitable; if prices do not recover, up to 50 000 jobs could be lost.

- South Africa has among the highest mining costs in the world, compared with foreign competitors. This is due to gold deposits which are deep underground; and lack of mechanization in the mines, because of reliance on cheap black labour.

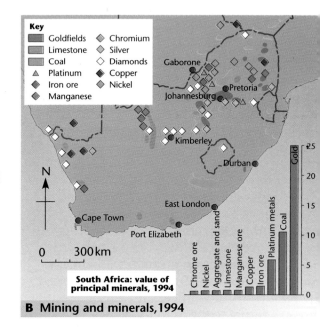

B Mining and minerals, 1994

Effects on people and communities

As the price of gold falls, mining companies and workers are faced with the threat of mines closing, unemployment and the decline of communities. For example, the Benoni Plant near Johannesburg closed down in July 1997. At its peak it employed 18 000 people. By 199? it had fewer than 2 000 workers.

Date	Production (tonnes)	Value (thousands Rand)
1920	253	91 212
1930	333	91 040
1940	436	235 981
1950	361	289 552
1960	665	536 019
1970	1 000	831 233
1980	672	10 369 275
1986	638	17 283 251
1996	300	5 650 432

A Gold production in South Africa, 1920–90

Supply of gold	Metric tons	%	Marketing	Demand for gold	Metric tons	%
Production:						
South Africa	621	40.4	Price $437	Jewellery	1 484	80.2
USA and Canada	334	21.7		Electronics and dentistry	183	9.9
Other	583	37.9		Other industrial uses	59	3.2
Total production	1 538	100.0		Medals and official coins	118	6.4
Recycled gold	258			Investment	6	0.3
Total world supply	2 120		1 850 tons	Total	1 850	100.0

C Production, marketing and use of gold, 1988

ommunities in many parts of the country
epend totally on mining for their livelihood.
ne economic and social effects of mine closure
ill be felt most in rural areas where mines are
ften the only source of income. Examples are
laces like Orkney in the North West and
irginia in the Free State. If the mines closed
nese would become ghost towns, with bars,
estaurants and shops forced to close.

is not only gold miners who are at risk.
very three of South Africa's 350 000 miners
upports at least one other person in industries
uch as explosives, steel, drilling machinery
nd engineering. Also, with over one-third of
ne population unemployed, every worker
upports on average between seven and ten
ependants. So any fall in employment in the
nines will have a drastic effect on the
conomy and on the ability of the government
o provide for its citizens.

ffects on the economy

outh Africa's gold production accounts for
bout 25 per cent of **GDP** and over 50 per cent
f export earnings. Any fall in output and
xport earnings will hit the country very badly.

he fortunes of the gold mining industry are
lso felt far away from the mines. Many
nigrant workers from Lesotho, Swaziland,
imbabwe and Mozambique have been made
nemployed from South African mines. They
ontributed up to 70 per cent of rural household
arnings in their home countries and they have
ttle prospect of finding new jobs.

D Work in a gold mine is uncomfortable, difficult and dangerous, and above all it is uncertain

FACT FILE

Gold mining

The price of gold has fallen rapidly. Between 1995 and 1998 the price has fallen by over 33 per cent to reach an all-time low. For South African companies it has been a disaster. JCI, the first black-controlled mining group was liquidated (closed for business) in April 1998.

Gold price

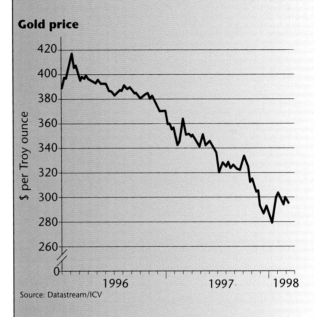

Source: Datastream/ICV

The mining industry has long been associated with diseases such as tuberculosis (TB). TB was not found in South Africa until the development of mining in the late nineteenth century. The mining authorities were able to exploit blacks as sources of cheap labour since there was little land available to blacks, and new taxes were placed on black farmers.

One reason why TB became such a common illness among blacks was that they were forced to live in huge compounds – massive single-sex hostels with thousands of blacks living in overcrowded conditions. The diet was monotonous – porridge, some meat and beef, but the working day and working conditions were poor. Work shifts of 10–12 hours were common – and, as the photo (left) shows, the work was very tiring, in hot damp conditions.

TB later spread from the mines to the **rural** areas (**homelands**) as returning **migrants** carried the disease with them.

▶ Why is energy important in South Africa?
▶ How has the government overcome its lack of energy resources?

South Africa has two sorts of energy problems, for families and for the country as a whole.

Family energy supply

For many black families, especially in rural areas, the problem is access to any sort of energy. When the Mandela government took over in 1994, about 3.6 million households, over 19 000 black schools and 2 000 clinics had no electricity. The government is working hard to put the situation right, but it will take years to connect the whole country to the electricity grid.

Meanwhile, each family uses an average of three to four tonnes of wood a year in their never-ending search for fuel. As we saw in chapter two, the vegetation does not recover in South Africa's fragile environment, so dustbowl conditions and desertification are created.

Energy for the country

South Africa has good supplies of coal, some good sites for **HEP** but no oil supplies (A, B). Also, much of the coal is soft, bituminous coal which has a low calorific (heat) value but a high ash content. However, the coal seams are thick and easily worked. This has led to widespread pollution (see pages 16–17). During the apartheid years the situation was made worse because the United Nations banned oil supplies to South Africa. One response was to build nuclear power stations. Another was to make oil from coal.

SASOL, a world first

South Africa has the world's biggest coal-to-oil **synthetic fuel** programme. Under apartheid, the South African Coal, Oil and Gas Corporation (SASOL) invented a process to turn solid coal into refined oil, hoping to beat restrictions on oil imports. The South African government hopes that the SASOL process will:

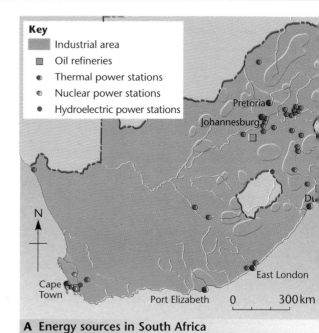

Key

▨	Industrial area
▣	Oil refineries
◉	Thermal power stations
◐	Nuclear power stations
●	Hydroelectric power stations

A Energy sources in South Africa

	1970	1992
Production	48.5	134.3
Imports	16.6	23.2
Exports	1.8	43.4
Consumption per person	2.2	2.5

(Millions of tonnes of coal equivalent)

B Energy in South Africa, 1970–92

- help solve the energy problem;
- be the foundation of a chemicals industry which can compete around the world;
- generate thousands of desperately needed jobs

The process by which SASOL makes liquid fuel also produces specialized chemicals. The fuel sells for about $200 (£1 = about US$1.5 in 1998) a tonne, but the chemicals can fetch as much as $1 000 a tonne. SASOL hopes to get 50 per cent of its income from chemicals by the end of the decade.

Despite its successes, there are also problems with this process:
- it wastes coal and greatly increases carbon emissions;
- processing synthetic fuels produces concentrated hazardous wastes, as well as sulphur and nitrogen oxides and hydrocarbons.

About 180 000 South Africans work in the chemicals industry as a whole, producing 5 per cent of gross domestic product. The industry could be improved by modernizing and investing in equipment, and training its workers. There are also problems such as high transport costs which make it difficult to export outside Africa.

C Making oil at SASOL's energy plant, Sasolburg

D For many South Africans firewood is an important source of energy

FACT FILE

Energy

South Africa has considerable amounts of energy **resources**, notably coal. However, it lacks oil and many people have limited access to sufficient energy resources. Coal accounts for about 80 per cent of energy consumption but for many people wood and rubbish is an important source of fuel to burn for heat. Coal has many uses: 52 per cent is used for electricity, 38 per cent for commerce and industry (including synthetic liquid fuels), 6 per cent for metallurgy and 3.5 per cent to households, and 1 per cent for mining and transport.

Renewable forms of energy (such as hydroelectric, solar and wind) have not been developed very much in South Africa. This is partly on account of their cost, but partly on account of the abundance and low cost of coal. Less than 5 per cent of the country's energy is supplied by renewable forms.

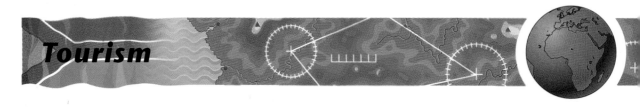

▶ **Why is tourism important to South Africa?**
▶ **What advantages and problems does tourism bring?**

International tourism

South Africa is described as 'a world in one country.' Following the 1994 elections, South Africa has become one of the world's fastest-growing tourist destinations (**A**). The majority of visitors are European although more people are coming from North America (**B**).

South Africa's attractions include the Kruger National Park, the scenic beauty of the Cape, hiking trails in the Drakensberg, beaches in Natal, the gold and diamond mines and, increasingly, tours of Soweto township near Johannesburg.

A government report in 1996 stated that 'tourism development in South Africa has largely been a missed opportunity. If South Africa's history had been different, it would probably have been one of the most visited places in the world.'

There is still room for expansion. Tourism accounts for 3 to 4 per cent of South Africa's GDP, compared with a world average of about 11 per cent. With gold mining in long-term decline, South Africa is desperately looking for an alternative economic activity to create jobs and bring in much needed foreign money. Tourism has been described as the most promising alternative.

Tourism still faces big problems:
• too few, overcrowded hotels;
• the high rate of crime in some areas.

Tourism inequalities

Although tourism benefits South Africa in some ways, it does not benefit everyone equally. Only an estimated 20 per cent of black families can afford to take a holiday in South Africa. Also much of the tourist infrastructure (for example

1990	300 000
1994	700 000
1995	800 000
2000 (est)	1 600 000

A The growth of overseas tourism, 1990–2000

UK and Ireland	244 860
Rest of Europe	442 679
North America	124 354
Central and South America	29 037
Australasia	59 951
Asia	129 400
Middle East	20 485
Indian Ocean Islands	11 073
Total	1 071 839

B Overseas visitors to South Africa, 1995

C An artificial beach on South Africa's south coast

hotels, airline companies, restaurants) are owned by white rather than black people. So many black people believe that the benefits of tourism mainly go to white people.

Although the government is keen to promote tourist development it has chosen to cut the tourism budget to put more money into welfare, education and housing.

Tourist chiefs want to develop South Africa as an upmarket tourist destination. They do not want to attract low budget package holidays, where holiday makers destroy the attractions they come to see. Already visitor numbers are limited in the Kruger National Park.

F Tourists on safari

D THE KRUGER NATIONAL PARK

The Kruger National Park is one of the most famous of South Africa's attractions. It has more wildlife species than any other park in Africa, due to its variety of habitats. The park has all the 'big five'. However, the large number of visitors can be a problem and there is increasing soil erosion and litter, mainly due to visitor pressure.

	Number of species
Trees	300
Fish	49
Amphibians	33
Reptiles	114
Birds	507
Mammals	147

E Species diversity in Kruger National Park

G Rhino, Kruger National Park

FACT FILE

Recent trends in tourism in South Africa
- There was an 11.4 per cent increase in the number of foreign tourists to South Africa in 1995.
- The largest increase (120 per cent) was in French visitors, following an advertising campaign on French public transport.
- South Africa's African visitors are growing slowly (0.5 per cent).
- The majority (over 75 per cent) of overseas tourists to South Africa are holiday makers, while business visitors, students and transit visitors (using South Africa to get somewhere else) made up the rest.
- The proportion of people using South Africa for a holiday is increasing.
- In 1995 approximately 4.5 million visitors went to South Africa.

- The relative value of South Africa's main tourist-sources is:

UK	15%
Germany	14%
France	4%
North America	10%
Asia	9%

Tourism is the world's most important industry – and many countries actively encourage it. Although there are many advantages – such as jobs, investment, foreign currency, there are serious questions about the environmental and cultural sustainability and acceptability of the increase in tourism.

Private game parks: making the best of South Africa's dry areas?

▶ **What is the best way to use dry areas?**
▶ **Should hunting be allowed?**

The Tarkuni Estate is located in the southern Kalahari Desert, 130 km from Kuruman in the Northern Cape. Springbok, a type of small antelope, are common there. But there are also some prized animals such as eland, kudu, and oryx.

Tarkuni Estate is the largest, privately-owned game reserve on the African continent. Its owner, Stephen Boler, is aware that land is becoming increasingly scarce as population increases and that people need more land for agriculture. But in many cases tourism, especially hunting, is more profitable, and it also has a valuable ecological role.

The argument for hunting
The management policy of the Tarkuni Estate is 'shoot to **cull**'(kill). Most of the 9 000 hectares are given over to wildlife breeding and ecotourism. On the rest of the land, hunters from Europe and North America are invited to pay to kill animals. Different animals receive different prices (figure B).

For hunters who have flown thousands of miles from Europe or North America the thrill of the hunt is a great attraction. But it results in the death of a wild animal. For many people, especially observers from the developed world, such killing is just wanton destruction – unnecessary killing for the sake of it.

As population increases in South Africa there is more need for farmland. This restricts the amount of land for wild animals. This means that some animals have to be culled in order to avoid overpopulation (when they wipe out their food supply and then starve themselves). According to the Tarkuni Estate it makes sense to let rich foreigners pay for the cost of conservation by letting them do the shooting.

Tarkuni Estate	
Land Area	1,036 km², varied terrain for rifle and bow hunting
Animals	40 species of 'trophy' game
Accommodation	3 and 5 star lodging
Staff	include resident biologist overseeing herd management
Tourist info.	in a disease–free zone, no malaria. Own Tarmac runway. Free transportation.

A Some facts about Tarkuni Estate

Jackal	$75
Ostrich	$300
Giraffe	$2 950
Roan (antelope)	$6 500
Buffalo	$6 000
White Rhino	$35 000

B The cost of culling

C Ecotourism allows tourists to get close to nature

D Translocation involves the movement of wildlife from its natural habitat to a designated area, like a game park

Ecotourism

There is some conflict with ecotourists. An ecotourist is someone who tries to experience and enjoy nature for its own sake. At nearby Tswalu, ecotourists watch the animals in their natural environment but do not try to kill them. On the other hand, many conservation groups are quite happy with culling. For example, the Worldwide Fund for Nature accepts culling (by tourists) provided it is sustainable, scientific and involves no cruelty, and there is no alternative that benefits local people.

Trophy hunting earns more money than tourism, which in turn earns more than farming. However, the biggest earner is from breeding rare animal species and selling surplus animals to other reserves.

FACT FILE

The growth of ecotourism

Ecotourism developed as a form of specialised, flexible tourism. It emerged because mass tourism was seen as having a negative impact upon the natural and social environment. At first, people who took an 'ecotourism' holiday were prepared to accept quite simple accommodation and facilities. This is sustainable and has little effect upon the environment. However, as a location becomes more popular and is marketed more, the number of tourists increases, causing more accommodation and improved facilities to be built. This is an unsustainable form of tourism as it destroys part of the environment and/or culture that tourists choose to visit.

South Africa and international trade

▶ What does South Africa import and export?
▶ How is South Africa's trade changing?

Overseas trade is buying and selling with other countries. **Imports** are the goods and services South Africa buys from other countries. These are mainly things the country cannot produce itself. **Exports** are the goods and services South Africa sells to other countries. The difference between them is called the **balance of trade**. If a country exports more than it imports, then it is earning more than it pays out (**A**).

South Africa trades with many countries. Two of its main trading partners are trading blocs, the **European Union (EU)** and the **Southern African Development Community (SADC)**. A trading bloc is a group of countries which agree to have free trade between them, with no restrictions or **tariffs** (taxes).

South Africa and Southern Africa

The Southern African Development Co-ordination Conference (SADCC) was formed in 1980 and became the Southern African Development Community in 1992. South Africa joined the community in 1994; there are now twelve member countries.

South Africa was keen to join SADC because of the advantages of being part of a trading bloc:
- exporters can reach a bigger market;
- the countries in the trading bloc have more bargaining power because they can act together;
- imports can be restricted by having tariffs on imports.

South Africa has a positive balance of trade with all the other members of SADC (**C**).

South Africa and the European Union

The Lome Convention is a treaty which governs trade relations between the EU and some of the world's poorest countries. The Convention is due to end in 2000. In the eyes of the EU, South Africa does not qualify for preferential trading conditions and European aid granted to other poorer Lome members. Southern European countries, led by Spain, are worried that South African exports would threaten their own agriculture and fisheries.

A A lot of South African wines are exported

IMPORTS	million rand
Primary products	
Food	1 060
Inedible raw materials	1 038
Manufactured goods	
Chemicals	3 828
Textiles	781
Metals and metal products	1 371
Machinery	8 476
Motor vehicles	3 082
All other manufactured goods	4 563
Other	4 469
Total	**28 672**

EXPORTS	million rand
Primary products	
Food	2 418
Metal ores	1 185
Diamonds*	3 547
Gold	17 807
Manufactured goods	
Chemicals	1 266
Metals and metal products	4 441
Machinery and transport equipment	957
Other	12 046
Total	**43 670**

*(excluding industrial diamonds)

B Imports and exports, 1994

EU exports to South Africa			EU imports from South Africa		
	1994 ECU (m)	Growth rate 1992–4 (%)		1994 ECU (m)	Growth rate 1992–4 (%)
Agricultural products	271	25.0	Agricultural products	813	–3.1
Industrial products	7 008	38.4	Industrial products	3 506	13.6
			Precious stones and minerals	2 338	–88.6
Total	7 279	37.8	Total	6 657	–26.6

(1 ECU = $1.2)

C EU exports to South Africa, 1994

	Rand (billion)	% of total
Nuclear reactors, boilers, machinery	11.8	24.5
Electrical machinery	6.8	14.0
Other unclassified goods	4.3	8.9
Vehicles and parts	4.1	8.6
Chemicals and chemical products	2.7	5.6
Optical, photographic, measuring equipment etc.	1.9	3.9
Plastics and plastic articles	1.6	3.3
Paper and paperboard	1.1	2.3

D South Africa exports to EU, 1994

FACT FILE

South Africa and international trade

South Africa is an obvious base for companies that want to take advantage of a regional market containing up to 250 million people.

South Africa is once again part of the southern Africa economic map. Moreover, it has the best transport and telecommunications **infrastructure** in Africa, it produces more electricity than the rest of Africa put together, and it has one-third of all of Africa's telephone lines.

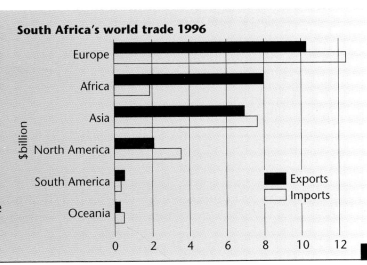

South Africa's world trade 1996

49

Black people developing the rural economy

▶ **What is the informal sector?**
▶ **What are black people doing to develop their communities?**

Although life is difficult for many black people and there is a history of injustice and inequality, there are many ways people have tried to improve their lifestyles and develop the community.

Informal businesses

The number of businesses owned by black people in South Africa is growing very fast. At first many were small-scale, informal activities, such as selling food, driving taxis, and small-scale manufacturing such as making bricks (photo **B**) This is called the 'informal economy' and is not controlled by strict taxes and laws.

Formal business development

Since the end of apartheid and the election of the new government in 1994, the economy has changed. There is a growing black middle class and many more black managers and industrialists in the formal economy. By 1996 black businesspeople had gained a huge increase in their share of South Africa's economic power. Some white-owned companies were transferred to black owners, and the companies were doing well.

Many businesses, black and white alike, have been affected by conditions outside South Africa. Rising competition and lower import tariffs have made foreign goods cheaper compared with South African goods. This has forced many businesses to close and caused widespread unemployment.

Taxi operators	100 000
Hawkers (street traders)	150 000
Small shopkeepers	50 000
Small backyard manufacturers	70 000
Others	130 000
Total	500 000

A Black-owned businesses in South Africa, 1995

Community Development in Makua, 1991

There are many more opportunities for business in urban areas than in rural areas,

B Brick making near Glenmore, Eastern Cape

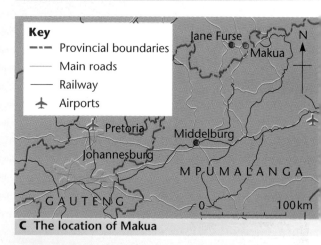

Key
- - - Provincial boundaries
— Main roads
— Railway
✈ Airports

C The location of Makua

D Intensive commercial development at Keiskammahoek, Eastern Cape

where consumers are very poor. But throughout South Africa there are many attempts by community groups to create jobs, improve living conditions and encourage sustainable development.

Domestic workers	26%
Gardeners	12%
Seamstresses	8%
Hawking	7%
Taxi driving	7%
Brewing/selling alcohol	5%
Other (labourers, cooks, wood collectors, car washers, bottle collectors, herbalists, hairdressers)	35%

E Main informal employment in South Africa, as a percentage of total workforce

F Dimbaza's CBD

An example of this is Makua village, where the Makua Women's Club decided to overcome the problems of unemployment and the shortage of housing by making bricks. Brick making is an activity usually controlled by men, and at first there was some resistance from local male builders who feared the women were trying to take over their profitable business. Instead, the brick making is part of a much wider development process. Brick making generates an income, and provides materials to build new, better housing. But men's resistance can be overcome, so it is essential for men and women to work together, rather than against each other.

Soil erosion in the region is another serious problem – without action food production in future would suffer. The Women's Club also organized tree-planting programmes. The trees will produce fruit and firewood and reduce soil erosion by wind and water.

One of the main problems is hunger. It is difficult to carry out these schemes when people are hungry and unmotivated. So the Women's Club has put a lot of work into increasing food production by cultivating more land, planting new seeds, carefully weeding and increased watering of crops. Farming has become more **labour-intensive**. The results are impressive, with new crops of carrots, pumpkins, sweet potato and maize.

One of the main strengths of these projects is that ordinary people carry them out with little money. However in rural areas a major problem is that many of the people with initiative and skills have already migrated in search of a better life in the city.

FACT FILE

Some common development terms

Bottom-up development involves local communities and local people. It is labour intensive and there is usually limited funding available. Common projects include building earthen dams and creating cottage industries.

Appropriate development is development that is culturally acceptable, technologically understandable and economically affordable. It is for and by the community using the community's own resources. It is a type of bottom-up or sustainable form of development.

Sustainable development aims to increase standards of living without destroying the environment, and to satisfy basic needs such as food supply and water.

Non-government organisations (NGOs) such as Oxfam, Save the Children and Cafod are mostly charities and are not allied to any political party. NGOs normally work with local communities and small groups, and they help with emergency relief.

5 UNEQUAL REGIONS

Measuring regional inequalities

▶ **What is development?**
▶ **How is it measured?**
▶ **How do levels of development vary across South Africa?**

Development is difficult to define. Development can be about improvements in:
- the economic growth in the country;
- peoples' standards of living;
- employment;
- health and nutrition;
- education;
- freedom and human rights;
- improved technology.

Most countries have inequalities in development between different regions. South Africa has contrasts in levels of development between regions, as well as striking inequalities between black and white people (see pages 26–27).

Some of these contrasts, like freedom and human rights, can be difficult to measure. Others, like GDP, are easy to measure but don't tell the whole picture about development.

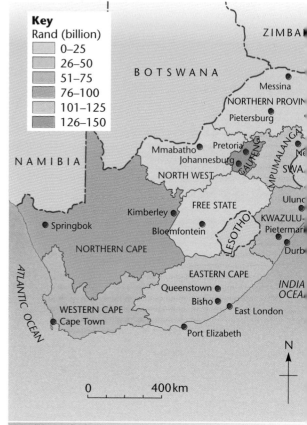

Key
Rand (billion)
- 0–25
- 26–50
- 51–75
- 76–100
- 101–125
- 126–150

ZIMBA

BOTSWANA

Messina

NORTHERN PROVIN

Pietersburg

NAMIBIA

Mmabatho ● Pretoria

Johannesburg

NORTH WEST

N

SWA

Ulunc

FREE STATE

Kimberley ●

KWAZULU-

● Springbok

Bloemfontein

Pietermar

Durb

NORTHERN CAPE

EASTERN CAPE

Queenstown ●

INDIA
OCEA

Bisho ●

WESTERN CAPE

East London

● Cape Town

Port Elizabeth

N

0   400 km

B Chloropleth map of GDP by province, 1994

A Contrasts in development: rubbish tips in the shadow of the CBD

Province	Population (million)	GDP per province (billion rand)	GDP per person (thousand rand)
Northern Province	5.4	14.7	1.9
North West	3.3	21.2	6.5
Gauteng	7.0	144.4	17.5
Mpumalanga	3.0	31.2	9.5
Northern Cape	0.7	80.0	9.2
Free State	2.8	23.7	7.8
KwaZulu-Natal	8.7	57.0	6.0
Western Cape	3.7	53.9	11.3
Eastern Cape	6.5	29.0	3.8

C Regional inequalities in South Africa, 1994

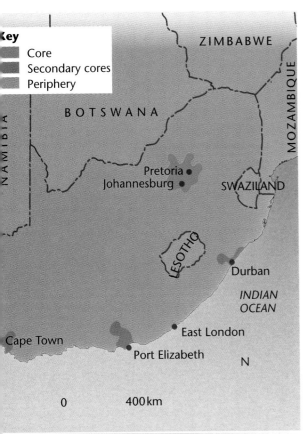

Key
- Core
- Secondary cores
- Periphery

ZIMBABWE

BOTSWANA

MOZAMBIQUE

NAMIBIA

Pretoria •
Johannesburg •

SWAZILAND

LESOTHO

Durban

INDIAN
OCEAN

Cape Town

East London

Port Elizabeth

N

0   400 km

**D Core/periphery model of regional inequalities in
South Africa**

For example, they don't include wealth produced in the informal economy, or unpaid work. Table **C** shows how GDP is produced in different regions of South Africa.

Core and periphery

One way to help understand differences in development between regions is to use the idea of core and periphery (**D**). **Core** regions are where there is much economic activity, especially industry and business; most of the nation's wealth is concentrated here. South Africa's core region is Gauteng, though there are other **secondary cores**. Away from the cores there are less prosperous areas: the **periphery**. Here there is less economic activity, and incomes and standards of living are lower.

The inequalities in wealth and development between the core regions and the periphery are a severe problem for South Africa. What makes the situation worse is that the core grows and develops at the expense of the periphery. We will investigate this in the next pages.

FACT FILE

Comparative data on race and inequality
As we have seen earlier there are racial inequalities as well as regional inequalities in

South Africa. The following diagrams show that the inequalities between blacks and whites in South Africa is much greater than in the USA.
ppp purchasing power parity
HDI Human Development Index

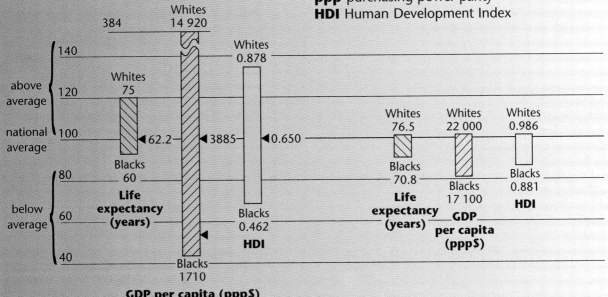

SOUTH AFRICA

Whites 384   Whites 14 920

Whites 0.878

Whites 75

62.2   3885   0.650

Blacks 60

Life expectancy (years)

Blacks 0.462
HDI

Blacks 1710
GDP per capita (ppp$)

USA

Whites 76.5
Whites 22 000
Whites 0.986

Blacks 70.8
Blacks 17 100
Blacks 0.881

Life expectancy (years)
GDP per capita (ppp$)
HDI

▶ **Where is South Africa's economic core?**
▶ **How and why has it become the core?**

South Africa's core region

As we saw on pages 52–53, South Africa has huge differences in levels of development between its regions. South Africa's core region is centred on the Johannesburg area, in Gauteng province. Gauteng covers only 1.5 per cent of South Africa's land area, but produces:

- 45 per cent of South Africa's manufacturing output;
- 45 per cent of trade;
- 55 per cent of financial sector earnings;
- 30 per cent of the country's employment;
- 40 per cent of the gross domestic product.

A further 30 per cent of GDP is produced by the other main cities (secondary cores) and together they account for about one-third of the population.

JOHANNESBURG

Johannesburg is South Africa's most famous and dynamic city, although it is not the capital (which is Pretoria) or the seat of government (which is Cape Town). But it is the most important economic centre in the country, and is probably the largest and most successful settlement in Africa south of the Sahara. The area contains 20 per cent of South Africa's population.

The area around Johannesburg contains the gold-bearing rocks which at one time were the world's richest deposit. The core has been built on this mining success. In the late nineteenth century, earnings from mining were invested in industry and the infrastructure.

The size of the gold resource meant that the Johannesburg area developed rapidly. Workers were needed for the fast growing mines and factories; these workers needed homes and spent their wages on other goods. In turn this created more jobs and led to more investment, attracting more workers. This is called the multiplier effect (**D** on page 57). Once started, it was difficult to stop the growth of Johannesburg.

So Johannesburg had an **initial advantage**, its goldfields, but its economy soon grew to include a wide range of industries and services.

A Downtown Johannesburg

B An aerial view of Johannesburg

Today this region is the economic heart of the country. But despite the economic success of Johannesburg and other parts of the core region, there are also problems. Some of these are the result of the core's success. They include:

- overcrowding in areas such as Hillbrow and Joubert Park;
- a shortage of housing, especially low-cost housing;
- rapid immigration of young people in search of work;
- poor quality housing in the townships and central Johannesburg. Up to two-and-a-half million people live in informal (shanty) housing;
- segregated populations, racial and tribal conflict.

C Johannesburg's skyline: it could be almost any CBD in the developed world

South Africa's periphery

▶ **What is the periphery?**
▶ **What problems of development does it have?**
▶ **What can be done to improve conditions there?**

In some ways, people living in parts of South Africa's periphery face similar problems to people in peripheral regions in other countries. Incomes and standards of living are low, compared with the core. The South African periphery faced special problems under apartheid because government policy was to starve the homelands of development. These areas are the most underdeveloped part of the periphery, with:
• 40 per cent of the population,
• 13 per cent of the land,
• 8.3 per cent of employment,
• 5 per cent of GDP.

Population problems
The policies of apartheid led to a very uneven age-structure in the homelands (**A**). Despite the lack of resources population densities were high. The core's wealth sucks young people away, hoping to make a living in the cities, making the periphery even more difficult to develop.

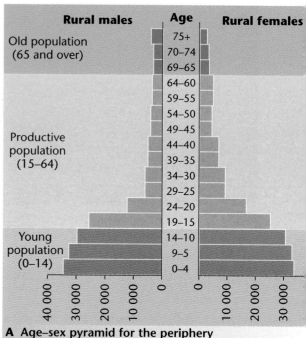

Rural males	Age	Rural females
Old population (65 and over)	75+	
	70–74	
	69–65	
	64–60	
	59–55	
	54–50	
	49–45	
Productive population (15–64)	44–40	
	39–35	
	34–30	
	29–25	
	24–20	
	19–15	
Young population (0–14)	14–10	
	9–5	
	0–4	

40 000 30 000 20 000 10 000 0 — 0 10 000 20 000 30 000

A Age–sex pyramid for the periphery

Jobs and the economy
The growing economy in the core acts like a magnet, attracting businesses there. In the periphery, agriculture is underdeveloped and much of the manufacturing is based on textiles and food processing (**B**).

Unemployment in the periphery is high. For people who are working in factories, domestic service and informal occupations wages can be very low. Many businesses are based on the exploitation of cheap labour.

B Many parts of the periphery are a very long distance from any large town. Some places are remote and inaccessible

C Many parts of the South African periphery lack substantial development, as shown by the lack of development in the CBD at Mdantsane

The Eastern Cape

The Eastern Cape, an underdeveloped part of the most depressed region in the country, sums up the problems of South Africa's periphery. It has raw materials, few towns and a poor infrastructure. It is a long way from the main markets in South Africa. Many people have migrated to the core, leaving behind a high proportion of children and old people.

Plans for development

The South African government's regional development policy plans to offset some of the inequalities between core and periphery. It aims to create jobs by focusing on **industrial development points** in and around the former homelands.

D THE MULTIPLIER EFFECT

Once the core began to grow, it attracted more people and economic activities. There were many benefits in locating here:
- being close to other businesses cut down transport costs;
- businesses could sell their products to the growing population;
- there were plenty of workers nearby.

The **multiplier effect** helps explain patterns of migration in South Africa in the 1950s and 1990s (pages 28–29). The core region's prosperity and jobs attracts migrants from the periphery. These are often young people who are more prepared to move, who may have children once they get to the city. So the core continues to grow and grow.

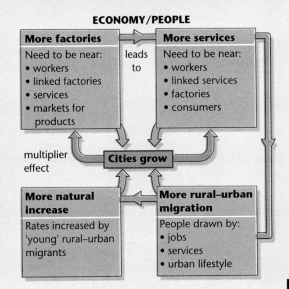

ECONOMY/PEOPLE

More factories
Need to be near:
- workers
- linked factories
- services
- markets for products

leads to

More services
Need to be near:
- workers
- linked services
- factories
- consumers

multiplier effect

Cities grow

More natural increase
Rates increased by 'young' rural–urban migrants

More rural–urban migration
People drawn by:
- jobs
- services
- urban lifestyle

The main site chosen for industrial development in the Eastern Cape was Dimbaza. The most important industry is clothing and textiles, with 60 per cent of jobs. Much of the workforce is female, especially in textile factories. Wages are very low and often do not provide enough of a household income.

The government provides **incentives** to attract industries. For example, industries setting up in Ciskei get:
- moving allowance;
- freedom from some taxes, reductions on others;
- electricity and transport grants;
- housing subsidies for managers;
- grants for every person employed.

In spite of government efforts, industrial development has been expensive and has not been a great success. The disadvantages of the periphery were too strong – many of the firms have closed or moved to the core.

Unless the government can find other ways of developing the periphery, more black people, especially the young and well educated, will migrate to big cities. It will become even less attractive for investors and regional inequalities will increase even more.

FACT FILE

The Eastern Cape and Dimbaza – an update
In the Eastern Cape most rural people have no choice but to walk up to 2 kilometres to collect water. Most have no sanitation, no electricity, no telephone and no work.

In Dimbaza 70 per cent of the adult population are unemployed. The town is a ghost town. In the centre of the town is a children's cemetery, mostly bearing infants under the age of two years. In the 1970s heavy storms washed away many of the graves, and little skeletons appeared at the bottom of the hill.

During the 1970s Dimbaza was a 'showcase of investment opportunity'. However, most of the investments have collapsed or gone elsewhere. Outside one of the few remaining factories queues of desperate men and women wait in the vain hope of a few hours' work.

Issues for the twenty-first century

▶ What hope does the future hold for South Africa's development?

At the end of the twentieth century, South Africa is changing rapidly and many people wonder how things will change after Nelson Mandela leaves office. The country faces a number of issues:

- those within South Africa;
- those in Southern Africa;
- those concerning South Africa and the global economy.

Issues in South Africa

1 Can South Africa tackle racial inequalities in: income; welfare; education; housing; health?
2 Can South Africa support its rapidly growing population?
3 Where will it find the money to create jobs and houses?
4 How will it cope with population growth in the twenty-first century?

In its favour South Africa has some big advantages:

- a talented, innovative population that has moved forward in a spirit of reconciliation since the new government was elected in 1994;
- the largest known mineral reserves in Africa;
- tremendous opportunities for tourism;
- the good will of many countries in the world.

South Africa and Southern Africa

1 Should South Africa concentrate on becoming a superpower in southern Africa or should it try to resolve its own problems within the country?
2 Could a Southern African trading bloc become as important as the European Union?
3 Would a **trading bloc** give the countries of Southern Africa a more powerful say in world politics?
4 South Africa is the richest country in Southern Africa. Will it end up having to spend money on its neighbours rather than its own people?

A The 'new' South Africa and the 'old': Thabo Nbeki, Nelson Mandela and F.W. de Klerk

5 Should South Africa compete with its neighbouring countries or co-operate with them?

To help it shape the future of Southern Africa, South Africa has the political, economic and financial resources to lead the region. Its leaders are experienced negotiators, and have shown how it is possible to overcome decades of discrimination before forming a government.

The new government has tried to follow a **capitalist** form of development which continues to create wealth rather than just spread it out. But there may be difficult choices: creating wealth or tackling inequalities.

B South Africa: the rainbow nation

outh Africa and the world

Is South Africa a developed country or a less developed country?

Should South Africa receive aid to help it develop?

How can South Africa develop in a sustainable way?

Should South Africa benefit from its large low-paid workforce and try to attract multinational companies?

outh Africa's economy has two parts; a small eveloped sector, and a less-developed sector which is much larger. This means that the ountry has experience and know-how but this eeds to be shared around.

C South Africa in the Olympics

South Africa is entitled to aid as much as any other country. However, trade is more important because it is a long-term process. South Africa has quite a healthy trading pattern – this will be useful in the future.

With a rapidly growing population, especially in overcrowded rural areas, South Africa has to adopt more sustainable practices. Years of discrimination have forced people to develop survival techniques. These can be developed into sustainable forms of agriculture, soil conservation and water conservation. These are another important basis for development in the twenty-first century.

South Africa is attractive to multinational companies because of its cheap labour force. But South Africa needs to build up industries for the 21st century based on people's skills.

FACT FILE

South Africa's achievements

Two of the main achievements of South Africa's government since achieving power in 1994 are political stability and the determination of the government to follow conservative economic policies rather than redistributing much of South Africa's wealth to the underclass. Now the government needs to open the economy to private investors (deregulation) and create a better image of South Africa abroad.

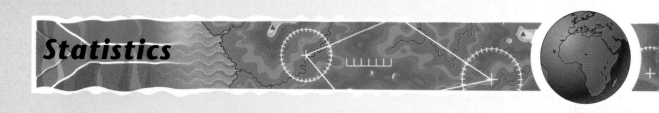

	BRAZIL	JAPAN	SOUTH AFRICA	UK	USA
population (millions)	159.1	125.1	44.0	58.3	263.6
Area (1 000 km^2)	8 512	378	1221	244	9809
Population density: (people per km^2)	19	332	36	241	28
Population growth (% per year)	2.1	0.3	3.0	0.2	1.1

Population

	BRAZIL	JAPAN	SOUTH AFRICA	UK	USA
Birth rate (per 1 000)	26	12	31	14	14
Death rate (per 1 000)	8	8	9	12	9
Infant mortality rate (per 100 live births)	57	5	62	8	8
Urban population	76	77	50	89	76
Fertility rate (no. of children per woman)	3	2	4	2	2
Age structure: 0–14	35	18	37	19	21
15–59	58	64	57	61	62
60+	7	17	6	21	17

Environment and economy

	BRAZIL	JAPAN	SOUTH AFRICA	UK	USA
Land use (%): arable	7	11	10	27	19
grass	22	2	67	46	25
forest	58	67	4	10	30
% workforce in: farming	25	7	13	2	3
industry	25	34	25	28	25
services	50	59	62	70	72
Average income (US$)	$2 920	$31 450	$2 900	$17 970	$24 750

Society and quality of life

	BRAZIL	JAPAN	SOUTH AFRICA	UK	USA
Energy used (tonnes/person/year)	0.44	4.74	2.49	5.4	10.74
Literacy (%)	81	99	81	99	99
Spending on education (as % of GNP)	3.7	5.0	3.8	5.3	7.0
Spending on military (as % of GNP)	1.2	1.0	3.0	4.0	5.3
Aid per person (US$)	1.2 received	90 given	4.9 received	50 given	38 given
United Nations HDI (out of 1.0)	0.80	0.94	0.65	0.92	0.92

Figures are for 1992–95. Source: *Philip's Geographical Digest* (United Nations, World Bank). The Human Development Index is worked out by the UN. It is a summary of national income, life expectancy, adult literacy and education. It is a measure of human progress. In 1992, the HDI ranged from 0.21 to 0.94.

Key statistics

Major features of relief
- the Kalahari plateau
- the plateau (Upper Karoo, Highveld, Bushveld)
- the Marginal Lands (lowveld, Great Karoo, Little Karoo)
- the Great Escarpment (Drakensberg, Snowberg)
- Coastal plains

Longest river: Orange and Vaal River 2340 km combined
Largest city: Johannesburg 6, 847, 000
Population density: 366 people per km sq
Capital cities: Pretoria, Cape Town and Blomfontein

Official languages

Official language	Share of population (%)
Zulu	22.4
Xhosa	18.3
Afrikaans	14.5
Pedi	9.1
English	8.4
Setswana	7.7
Sesotho	6.4
Tsonga	3.7
Siswati	3.1
Venda	1.7
Ndebele	0.7
Other languages	4.0

Religions

Christian 78% Non-Christian 22%
Roman Catholic 8%, Dutch Reformed Church 11%, Methodist 6%, Zion Christian Church 5%, Black Independent churches 17%
Muslims 1.2%, Hindus 2%

Economic indicators

World GNP ranking 31st
GNP/capita $2520
Inflation 5%
Unemployment 30%

Exports		Imports	
Netherlands	5%	Japan	10%
Japan	6%	USA	11%
UK	8%	UK	12%
Switzerland	9%	Germany	20%
Other	72%	Other	47%

Crime rate

Murders per 1000 population	
South Africa	109
Australia	2
USA	9
UK	3

Value of principal minerals

Gold	R25 million
Coal	R10 million
Platinum metals	R 6 million
Iron ore	R2 million
Copper	R2 million
Manganese ore	R1 million
Limestone	R 1 million
Aggregates and sand	R 1 million
Nickel	R 1 million
Chrome ores	R 1 million

Value and sales of major industries

Processed food	R29 million
Chemicals	R23 million
Machinery	R18 million
Vehicles	R17 million
Basic metals	R 17 million
Beverages and tobacco	R14 million
Metal products	R13 million
Petroleum products	R 13 million

Communications and media				
	South Africa	Australia	UK	USA
Mail posted (letters per person)	13.1	220	287	664
Telephones per 1000 people	146	487	446	515
TV sets per 1000 people	101	475	360	927
Daily newspapers per 1000 people	35	n/a	383	240

Note: The names of mountain ranges in maps are reproduced here in the original Afrikaans, where no convention exists for an English translation. Thus, the Afrikaans word 'berg' (sing.) or 'berge' (pl.) literally means 'mountain(s)'.

accessibility the centrality of a location – how easy is it to reach

adult literacy the percentage of adults that can read and write

altitude height of the land – it has an important influence on climate, vegetation and agriculture

apartheid a system of racial discrimination whereby the white minority had large advantages over the black population. The apartheid system created homelands for blacks, and there was also discrimination at an urban level (townships) and at a small-scale (facilities were segregated)

apartheid city a city divided both geographically and socially along the lines of apartheid

balance of trade the balance between a country's exports and imports; a positive balance means that exports are greater than imports

birth rate the number of live births per thousand population

bushveld a type of vegetation consisting of bushes, small trees and grass

capitalist a form of economic development where individual industrialists (or companies) exploit raw materials and workers to make a profit

check-dams small-scale earth or stone dams usually built by local communities to hold water and prevent soil erosion

colonists the earliest overseas migrants who moved into an area

colony a country that has been taken under the political and economic control of another country. Most 'colonies' were developing countries; the colonial powers were developed countries

commercial farms farms that produce goods to sell – their aim is to make a profit

condenses conversion of moisture from a gas to a liquid

convection storms thunder storms caused by the rising of warm air

core the core is the economic centre of the country, vibrant, rich in resources and showing growth, compared with a disadvantaged, depressed periphery, lacking in resources and growth

cull controlled killing of animals to keep their numbers down

death rate the number of deaths per thousand of population

deforestation removal of trees (and other vegetation) for farming, fuelwood and timber resources

desertification the spread of desert conditions into non-desert areas

diguettes small-scale dams

discrimination unequal treatment – favouritism for some but injustices for others

distribution where things are located/found

drought a long-term decline in water availability

emigrated someone who has left an area

European Union (EU) a group of countries in Western Europe which have close economical and political links and are a major trading partner with South Africa

exports goods or services that are sold by one country to another

formal economy the official part of the economy – businesses governed by laws and regulation

Gross Domestic Product (GDP) the value of goods produced in a country over a year

Gross National Product (GNP) the value of goods produced in a country over a year, plus income from services, tourism, investment and so on

gullies steep, narrow, deep channels created by water flowing over a surface

Highveld see veld

homelands areas set aside for black people under apartheid. Most were peripheral, isolated and fragmented pieces of land with very high population density

humid areas that are wet

hydro electric power (HEP) the use of water to generate power

immigrants people who move into an area or country

imports goods and services that one country buys from another

incentives attractions such as money, grants, factories and subsidies provided by the government to attract industry

industrial development points areas for industrial growth, located in the former homelands and/or distant from the main metropolitan areas

infant mortality rate the number of deaths in infants under the age of one year per thousand live births. This is usually expressed as the Infant Mortality Rate (IMR)

influx control policies aimed at controlling the movement of black people and their number in urban areas

informal economy unofficial jobs and businesses, e.g. domestic work, gardening, operating taxis and selling food

infrastructure the built environment, including roads, rail, housing, factories, water supplies, energy supplies and so on

initial advantage a feature such as a raw material that gives a location an advantage over other areas

irrigation water used to farm dry areas

labour-intensive large inputs of human labour – rather than machinery – to perform a task, e.g. farming or industry

latitude the position of a place north or south of the Equator

life expectancy the number of years that a person is expected to live for

locations another term for townships

longitude the position of a place east or west of Greenwich (London)

Mediterranean climate a climate with warm wet winters and hot dry summers

migrant labourers black and 'coloured' workers who worked away from home in mines and factories. They were often away from home for up to a year

migrated/migration a change in permanent residence

Minimum Living Level a level below which it is impossible to live/survive

multiplier effect the process where a growth area attracts investment and migrants and improves its advantages even (also known as cumulative causation)

natural hazards natural events which endanger the loss of life, property or livelihood

natural increase population growth where birth rates are greater than death rates

neonatal the first four weeks of life

NIC Newly Industrialising Country, for example, Korea and Malaysia, with a high percentage of the workforce employed in manufacturing, and a high percentage of exports from manufacturing

overgrazed loss of vegetation eaten by domestic and wild animals

payment in kind payment on farms by food or wine rather than wages

perception what people believe exists, rather than what actually exists

perinatal from the fourth week after conception to the first week after birth

periphery on the edge; away from the centre

peri-urban a large sprawling settlement lacking in most urban amenities such as jobs and basic services, usually on the edge of an urban area

pesticides chemicals used to destroy pests

plateau an area of flat land at high altitude

population composition a description of the population – normally the age–sex structure

population densities the number of people per km^2 – how many in an area

population distribution the actual location of people – where they are

population pressure the stresses placed upon the enviroment (and resources) by population growth

post-apartheid city the new urban form resulting from the collapse of the apartheid system

productivity a measure of how much is produced – commonly used in farming (yields/ha) or industry

raw material any natural resource which can be used, e.g. gold, coal, cotton

relief the effect of the altitude (height) or topography (shape) of the land

relief rainfall rain that is formed when air is forced to rise over high ground

reserves rural areas set aside by whites for black people to live in. These were peripheral, less developed parts of South Africa, away from economic centres. Later they became homelands

resettlement schemes the forced removal of black people and their 'resettlement' in homelands and periurban areas – this was a policy of the apartheid era

resource anything that is valuable e.g. gold, soil, diamonds, water, land

run-off rain water and flash floods that run over the land's surface

sanctions impositions planted on South Africa in order to put pressure on the former government to reform its ideas

secondary cores important urban industrial area – but not as dominant as the main core area

segregation the enforced separation of people of different races

semi-arid/semi-arid areas areas which receive about 350–500 mm of rain each year with seasonal drought

shebeens illegal drinking houses

soil erosion the removal of soil by water and wind at a rate greater than soil is being created

soil degradation a decline in the quantity (amount) or quality (fertility) of soil

South African Development Community (SADC) a collection of countries in Southern Africa which have close economic and trade links

subsistence farms farms which grow food for their own needs – not to sell

sub-tropical latitudes around 25°–35° either side of the Equator

synthetic fuel fuels made by the conversion of one material to another e.g. from coal to oil

tariffs taxes placed upon imports to make them more expensive and make home goods more competitive

trading blocs a group of countries that have protected access to an internal market, for example, the EU countries can trade within themselves – a market of 370 million people

township separate area of generally low-quality housing reserved for black people, 'coloureds' or Asian people

toxic poisonous

toxic heavy metals concentrations of toxic metals in the soil e.g. lead, zinc, mercury, cadmium

urban/urbanized where many people live in large built up areas, with a high proportion of manufacturing and service jobs

urbanization an increase in the proportion of population living in urban or peri-urban areas

veld grassland

vlei(s) grassland

Index

Bold type refers to terms included in the glossary Italic type refers to photographs or maps.

African National Congress (ANC) 9
agriculture 10, 15, 16, 18, 19, 20, 21, 26, 28, 32, 36–7, 51, 56
   commercial farming 15, 32, 36, *36*, *37*
   subsistence farming 36, *36*
aid 59, 60
altitude 10, 12
apartheid 8–9, 16, 20, 22, 28, 35, 42, 55, 56

birth and death rates 24, 25, 27, 60
black population 8, 22, 25, 27–32, 34–39, 41, 42, 44, 50–51, 53

Cape Town 12, 14, *30*, 54
Ciskei 20, 29, 37, 57
cities 30–31
climate 4, 10, 12–13, *13*, 21
coal 16, 17, 42, 43
communications 34, 49, 61
core regions 53, *53*, 54–55, 56, 57
crime 6, 34, 38, 61

dams 15, 19, *19*
deforestation 16, 19
Demographic Transition Model (DTM) 25
desertification 18–19, 42
development 51–53, 59
   capitalist development 58
   core regions 53, *53*, 54–55, 56, 57
   periphery 53, *53*, 56-57, *56*
   policy 57
diamond mining 28, 40
discrimination 7, 8, 28, 58, 59
diseases 27, 34, 41
drought 14, 15, 18, *18*, 19, 20, *21*
drylands 19
Durban 12, 13, 23, 27, 35

Eastern Cape 7, 8, 10, *31*, 57
economy 38, 39, 41, 44, 50–51, 56, 59, 60, 61
   formal economy 38, 50
   informal economy 38, 50, *50*, 51
ecotourism *46*, 47
education 26, 27, 60
elections 9
emigration 28
employment/unemployment 8, 23, 28, 34, 38, 40, 41, 56, 57, 60
environmental problems 16–17, 34
European Union (EU) 48

farming *see* agriculture
floods 12, 14, *14*, 15, 16
food production 18, 19, 37, 51

game parks 46–47, *46*
gold mining 28, 40–41, *41*, 54
Great Escarpment 11

Gross Domestic Product (GDP) 39, 41, 43, 44, 52, *52*, 53, 54
Gross National Product (GNP) 26, 61

homelands 8, *9*, 16, 20, 22, 26, 28, 36, 56
housing 7, 8, *8*, *17*, *26*, 31, *31*, 32, 34, 35, 55
human development 26–27, *27*
hydroelectric power 15, 42, 43

import tariffs 50
imports and exports 36, 41, 48, 49, 61
income 27, 34, 35, 37, 60
industry 16, 17, 28, 38-39, *38*, 39, 40–43, 54, 56, 57, 61
infant mortality 22, 23, 24, 27
Infant Mortality Rate (IMR) 27, 60
irrigation 15, 20

Johannesburg 4, 6, 12, 31, 54–55, *54*, *55*

land use 20, 60
languages 23, 61
latitude and longitude 4
life expectancy 22, 23, 25, 26, 27
locations *see* townships

Mandela, Nelson 8, 9, 58, *58*
marginal lands 11, 21
migration 8, 20, 23, 24, 28–29, *28*, *29*, 31, 41, 51, 57
mineral resources 38, 58, 61
Minimum Living Level 27
mining industries 16, 17, 28, 40–41, *40*, *41*, 54
mountain ranges 10, 11

National Party 8, 28
non-government organisations (NGOs) 51
Northern Cape 4

ocean currents 13
oil 16, 42, *43*
overgrazing 19, 20, *21*, 36

peri-urban settlements 8, 27, 30, 31
peripheral regions 56–57, *56*
plateau 10, 11, 15
political stability 59
pollution 16, *16*, 17, *17*, 34, 42, 43
population 8, 22–25, 60
   densities 23, *23*, 56, 60
   groups 22, 23
   growth 19, *21*, 22, *23*, 24–25, 34, 39, 58, 60
post-apartheid cities 30
poverty 20, 24, 27, 28
Pretoria 4, 54
provinces 4, *5*

racial inequalities 25, 27, 31, 35, 53, 58
   see also apartheid
rainfall 10, *10*, *11*, 12, 13, 15, 18, 20, 21, 23
regional inequalities 52–53, *53*
relief features *4*, *5*, 10–11, *10*, *11*, 32, 61
religions 61

reserves 28
resettlement schemes 8, *8*
rivers 14, *14*, 61
rural areas 32-33, 50-51

sanctions 9
segregation 8, 30, 55
soil degradation 16, 19, 20
soil erosion 12, 16, 20, 21, 36, 45, 51
South African Development Community (SADC) 48
Soweto 44
sport 6, *6*, *59*

telecommunications 49
temperatures 10, *11*, 12, 13, 20
tourism 44–45, 58
townships 6, 8, *8*, 16, 17, *17*, 22, 28, 30, *30*, 32, 34–35, 38, 55
trade 48–49, 58, 59
trading blocs 48, 58

United Nations 42
urbanization 30–31

vegetation 4, *11*, 20, 21

white population 22, 25, 27, 28, 31, 36, 37, 53
wildlife 6, 6, 45–47, *45–47*